"Jenny beckons readers to normalize allyship rather than leave it to a few, summoning the privileged to be part of the answer and not the problem. Without a lick of lip service, she goes first, grappling with how racism has been laced through her own story, all the while inviting readers to a place of advocacy and allyship that will lead to the flourishing of all God's children."

Tiffany Bluhm, author of *Prey Tell: Why We Silence Women Who Tell the Truth and How Everyone Can Speak Up*

"Jenny Booth Potter simultaneously acknowledges the emotional work White people must do to reckon with racism and injustice while refusing to accept White excuses, for herself or her readers. By sharing her story, she challenges us to start the lifelong work of dismantling White supremacy in society and in ourselves."

Blake Chastain, host of the *Exvangelical* podcast

"Jesus' call to justice is transformative—and has major implications on how we raise children, love neighbors, approach work, and embrace worship. In this historical and deeply personal book, Jenny Booth Potter weaves her experiences into a broader examination of racial injustice. Jenny is a gifted truth teller, sharing her imperfections to help White Christians like me reckon with sins of racism past and present. Jenny held a mirror to my soul, inviting me to examine my complicity, and I'm grateful for it. This book won't shame you, but it'll push you. Let it propel you beyond complacency and into God's call to embody antiracism in your everyday life."

Kayla Craig, author of *To Light Their Way* and creator of *Liturgies for Parents*

"It takes the most brave and generous souls among us to open up their lives and invite us along. As an ally and seasoned practitioner, Jenny Potter is undeniably one such soul. With striking vulnerability and sincere hope, she tells stories and unfolds memories that compel her readers to make the pursuit of antiracism the only viable option for a world of justice and mutual flourishing for us all."

Ashlee Eiland, co–lead pastor of Mars Hill Bible Church and author of *Human(Kind)*

"In *Doing Nothing Is No Longer an Option*, Jenny is doing some much-needed, patient guidance for people that w~~ant to 'get it' when it comes to~~ doing antiracism."

Andre Henry, columnist for Religion News Ser~~v~~
Friends I Couldn't Keep

T0054062

"As a Black woman, it is difficult for me to fathom anyone taking a backseat (or no seat at all) in the continued fight for racial equity and justice. Yet for too many White individuals, particularly White Christians, that's often the default response. In *Doing Nothing Is No Longer an Option*, Jenny Booth Potter writes directly to this audience in an honest and practical way, addressing this reality head-on. Starting with her own antiracist journey, there's no sugarcoating the challenges, missteps, and discomfort Jenny has encountered. But for those who are ready to self-examine, engage, and act, her words are a clarion call that is necessary and worth it."

Patricia A. Taylor, writer and antiracism educator

"With honesty and humility, Jenny Booth Potter takes readers on a journey of awakening to the layers of racism that pervade every sector of society as well as recognizing her own passive and active participation in it. This book gives other White women permission to confess their own racism and refuse passivity, instead leaning in to the lifelong work of dismantling racist strongholds in their own lives and in the world."

Katelyn Beaty, author, journalist, and editor

"I think mistakes (or, as I like to call them, 'pluck-ups') can be the source of some of life's greatest lessons. When, especially in the face of our pluck-ups, we choose curiosity over criticism, our mistakes and wrong turns can be some of our greatest teachers. As a White woman raising White sons myself, I relate to so much of Jenny's story, and I am grateful for her invitation to keep going in the pursuit of justice—even when the fear of failure can feel paralyzing. This book is a powerful invitation, and I'm so thankful it exists . . . because I am convinced, now more than ever, that doing nothing is no longer an option!"

Liz Forkin Bohannon, cofounder and CEO of Sseko Designs

DOING NOTHING IS NO LONGER AN OPTION

ONE WOMAN'S JOURNEY INTO EVERYDAY ANTIRACISM

JENNY BOOTH POTTER

FOREWORD BY **AUSTIN CHANNING BROWN**

An imprint of InterVarsity Press
Downers Grove, Illinois

InterVarsity Press
P.O. Box 1400 | Downers Grove, IL 60515-1426
ivpress.com | email@ivpress.com

InterVarsity Press® is a resource publishing division of InterVarsity Christian Fellowship/USA®. For more information, visit intervarsity.org.

Scripture quotations, unless otherwise noted, are from The Holy Bible, English Standard Version, copyright © 2001 by Crossway Bibles, a division of Good News Publishers. Used by permission. All rights reserved.

While any stories in this book are true, some names and identifying information may have been changed to protect the privacy of individuals.

Published in association with The Bindery Agency, www.theBinderyAgency.com.

The publisher cannot verify the accuracy or functionality of website URLs used in this book beyond the date of publication.

Cover design and image composite: David Fassett
Interior design: Jeanna Wiggins

ISBN 978-1-5140-0000-7 (print) | ISBN 978-1-5140-0001-4 (digital)

Printed in the United States of America ♾

Library of Congress Cataloging-in-Publication Data
Names: Potter, Jenny Booth, 1982- author.
Title: Doing nothing is no longer an option : one woman's journey into
    everyday antiracism / Jenny Booth Potter.
Description: Downers Grove, IL : InterVarsity Press, [2022] | Includes
    bibliographical references.
Identifiers: LCCN 2022024552 (print) | LCCN 2022024553 (ebook) | ISBN
    9781514000007 (paperback) | ISBN 9781514000014 (ebook)
Subjects: LCSH: Social justice–United States. | Anti-racism–United
    States. | Social change–United States.
Classification: LCC HM671 .P657 2022 (print) | LCC HM671 (ebook) | DDC
    303.3/72–dc23/eng/20220613
LC record available at https://lccn.loc.gov/2022024552
LC ebook record available at https://lccn.loc.gov/2022024553

29 28 27 26 25 24 23 22 | 9 8 7 6 5 4 3 2 1

To my parents – Ed and Becky

And for my boys – John, Elliot, and Milo

CONTENTS

FOREWORD

Austin Channing Brown

I WILL NEVER FORGET THE MOMENT JENNY BOOTH POTTER shifted from being my friend to my accomplice and partner in the pursuit of racial justice. We were on a trip with forty of our college peers to learn about America's racial history. But things weren't going well. Our group had dissolved into a muddy puddle of tears, hurt, and hopelessness.

Then came Jenny's voice.

Side-stepping defensiveness and instead embracing the pain of our racial history, she believed we could make a difference if only we confront our past . . . *and* our present. When she spoke the words *Doing nothing is no longer an option for me*, Jenny was speaking for herself, but she was also naming for me the vocation forming in my soul. Because as she said those words, I knew that I too would commit the rest of my life to antiracism work. There was no turning back. And I felt an instant and deep connection with her.

What I didn't know was how deep our connection in this work would be. That connection has survived not just our college years, but two decades worth of antiracism projects together. From demanding budgets to raising money, from creating curriculum to teaching hundreds, from being verbally assaulted to being gaslit, we have fought the good fight together.

When I give a lecture on racial justice, Black people ask me how I know when someone is an ally. It's a question born out of deep disappointment—of high hopes that a friend had become an ally, only to experience heartbreak when they walk away. But whenever I am asked this question about allies, I find myself describing Jenny.

You want someone who is committed—who won't walk away when coworkers start calling you *toxic* or *divisive*. You want someone who is teachable—who is always learning on their own without prodding or pushing from an external source. You want someone who is willing to step in when you're tired or sick or it's too dangerous for you to speak up. You want someone who is in it with you from beginning to end. Jenny has been all of those things to me and more.

Jenny will be the first to tell you that she hasn't gotten everything right. This book is not her ode to herself. Instead it is a peek inside her own journey, as a White woman who refuses to give up on her promise to keep going. Even when it's hard.

Inside these pages you will find an honest account of what it costs to move beyond performative allyship and get into the fight for justice. If you, as a White person, feel compelled to move off the sidelines and get into the fight for justice, but are unsure about how to begin your journey, there is no one I trust more to walk beside you than my friend Jenny.

And if you are a Black person, this book is not *for* you. But please feel free to hand this out to the White people in your life so you can stop accepting a gajillion coffee dates every time there is a racial uproar. You can trust Jenny to tell the truth so you can go about your day.

INTRODUCTION

Toni Morrison said, "The function of freedom is to free someone else," and if you are no longer wracked or in bondage to a person or a way of life, tell your story. Risk freeing someone else. Not everyone will be glad that you did. Members of your family and other critics may wish you had kept your secrets. Oh, well, what are you going to do? Get it all down. Let it pour out . . .

ANNE LAMOTT

I HAVE SPENT NEARLY TWENTY YEARS as a professional storyteller. At the start of my career, I served at nonprofits and helped craft stories of change and hope that could be shared in grant proposals, marketing materials, and at annual galas. Later, as a video producer for a large suburban megachurch, I conveyed beautiful and sometimes dramatic stories of redemption that played on huge screens in the church's main auditorium or showed up as social media posts across the small screen of someone's phone. And now I am one of the cofounders for Herself Media, a company dedicated to producing stories of Black girl/womanhood with joy and dignity. We are convinced that the "story is queen" and it is our job to "serve the queen."

I believe in the power of story—that if you want to create a space for connection, an opportunity for empathy, or the chance to change a mind or heart, you set aside the statistics and data for a moment and find the story of a person. I could easily tell you about the poor water conditions in a community in the Dominican Republic, but how much better is it to hear about a pastor named Maria who saw this problem and decided to open a water purification tank serving her neighborhood? Hearing Maria's story allows you to hear about the families whose children no longer get sick from dirty water or the young man who is able to pay for his education through the money he makes transporting the water.

It was at the megachurch job where I learned not only about the power of story but also the rhythm needed to tell a good story—the elements that alone are isolated but when threaded together create a narrative with highs and lows, challenges and overcomings. In his screenwriting book *Save The Cat!*, author Blake Snyder outlines the story beats or moments that move a story forward to create a compelling structure in many of the films and books we love. The beginning of every story (say, *The Wizard of Oz*) using this blueprint includes a scene that shows a "before" of the main character/hero (Dorothy on her family's farm in Kansas), then states the theme ("Somewhere Over the Rainbow"), sets up the problem (a tornado takes Dorothy out of Kansas), and explores the catalyst for change and what direction the hero will take next (Dorothy decides to follow the yellow brick road to the Emerald City). It is usually after the hero moves in a new direction that she meets a new character who serves as a guide or an expert (Dorothy meets the Scarecrow) to help the hero learn a lesson.

I can see this order of scenes as I reflect back on my own story: a long time of a life lived "before," a clear catalyst for change, and companions and guides on my journey. You see, I'm a storyteller, but I've often preferred to tell other people's stories for mainly one reason: I am not an expert. And perhaps a second: I am no one's hero. Much of my work as a White woman pursuing antiracism in my own life has been to remove myself from the center of things as much as I possibly can. I have repeated to myself, "Your story (i.e., the story of White people) has been told" over and over again. So how is it that you are holding this book in your hands?

I wrote this book because I think we need *more* examples, not *less*, of White people navigating, learning, unlearning, trying, messing up, and rejecting the desire for perfection in one's pursuit of racial justice. I did *not* do this to show off how much I know or to prove how exceptional of a White person I am—quite the opposite. There are parts of my story that I am ashamed of, parts that I wish I could undo or redo or forget ever happened. There are parts of my story where incredible learning happened, but it came at a cost: most often it cost the Black people and other people of color who either learned alongside me or taught me through their own experiences and from their own pain. There were trips I went on and experiences I had in which my feelings and understanding as a White person were often centered, where the hope was that I would come away from the experience changed. And I really did. But I don't want to convey that the ends justify the means. The means matter.

I wrote this book because I don't think we can eliminate isms of any kind—rac*ism*, sex*ism*, Christian national*ism*, class*ism*, able*ism*—without those who benefit most from them actively pursuing their elimination. As a White woman in the United States, I have benefited my entire life from racism. Nearly all those advantages were given to me; I did not have to pursue them. However, that in no way absolves me from my access to these societal leg ups.

I wrote this book because I want to live in a world where White people get better at questioning our own history and do a better job of interrogating ourselves, resulting in a better life for everyone.

I wrote this book because I hope it leads you to read books by women of color. Please don't let my book be the last one you read on this subject.

I wrote this book to introduce you directly and indirectly to people I am learning from.

I wrote this book because I have found a fuller version of my own humanity in the pursuit of antiracism. I have found my personal faith deepen and widen.

I wrote this book because there is so much pain and harm and violence and oppression occurring right now, and if there is a chance my words can be even a tiny part of the healing or point to some solutions to these atrocities, I might never stop writing.

I wrote this book because I believe a lot of my experiences—in the church, as a parent, as a colleague and friend—are not unique to just me. I'm excited to hear how our journeys overlap.

I wrote much of this book in the fall and winter of 2020, after the murders of George Floyd, Breonna Taylor, Ahmaud Arbery, and too many more. It was a time when ideas and concepts and terms were being discussed in many circles across the world with hypervisibility and deep urgency. One night in the weeks following George Floyd's murder, a dear friend called me, overwhelmed by all she was reading and learning and processing. I told her that she was trying to make up for an entire lifetime in just a few weeks—digging out old ideas and replacing them with new ones. "This process is like learning a new language—it takes time, and saying the wrong thing and messing up and learning from the mistakes are part of getting better." Finally, I reminded her that you can't get better at a new language without saying it *out loud*, so she'd need to find others to talk with. "Don't go at it alone. Find someone to walk this road with you."

I think too many of us are trying to do the work of antiracism on our own. The recovery community has modeled the importance of doing work together and having someone who has been down the path of addiction and opted for the daily choice of recovery, someone who walks alongside others on the journey with great empathy. So in that spirit, "My name is Jenny and I'm a racist in recovery. I know what it's like to start recognizing destructive and harmful ways of living as a White person. You are not alone." If you are up for it, I would love to be your sponsor and travel some of this journey together.

A few notes before we begin. First, you might have noticed that I've capitalized not just *Black* and other ethnic designations throughout the book, but also *White*. I'm leaning on what I've learned from sociologist and author Eve L. Ewing. She writes that when we limit *white* to just a description of skin color, we "run the risk of reinforcing the dangerous myth that White people in America do not have a racial identity. . . . White people get to be only normal, neutral, or without any race at all, while the rest of us are saddled with this unpleasant business of being racialized." Capitalizing *White* is one simple way of challenging that myth.

And second, to quote Oscar Wilde, "books are never finished, they are merely abandoned." This book is not finished because I am not finished. My journey hasn't ended; these pages serve as a time capsule for my life. That used to scare me—that I would share a version of my story I will look back at in a month, a year, a decade, and not fully want to claim. That I might even be a tad embarrassed by, because I will have grown in my knowing and unlearning when this book enters your world. But if I am going to share my story, I must surrender. I must release the desire to stand over you telling you all the things I would have changed since this book was printed. Instead, I will choose to celebrate where I am at in my journey, the many years I have spent traveling down this road, and the path that awaits me in the future. And I will always be thankful that you decided to join me at this exact moment, wherever you find yourself on your own journey.

Now, let's get to some stories.

1

WHITE GUILTY GIRL

*No one ever talks about the moment you found out that you
were white. Or the moment you found out you were Black.
That's a profound revelation. The minute you find that out,
something happens. You have to renegotiate everything.*

TONI MORRISON

"I WANT TO DO MORE THAN SMILE at Black people when I pass them on the sidewalk," I said earnestly to the woman seated on the couch across from me.

We were in her basement office, I was twenty years old, a junior in college, and had just made it to the interview round for a trip my university sponsored each year called Sankofa. *Sankofa* (SAHN-koh-fah) is a word in the Twi language of Ghana that often translates to "looking back to move forward." Once accepted, I would be one of forty students who left Chicago, boarding a bus to the South, for a deeper dive into the racial history of our country, gaining a deeper awareness and understanding primarily of the Black and White experiences and histories in the United States.

During our sophomore year, one of my closest friends, Megan, had gone on the trip. It was a powerful, important experience for her and it changed so many perspectives she had held her whole life. Megan was a White girl from Minnesota who had spent much of her childhood as a missionary kid in Bolivia, so I thought maybe it was a trip for people like her—people who had lots of crosscultural experiences or spoke a language besides English or had some reason to willingly step into an experience that at the time felt optional to me. My crosscultural experiences consisted of taking German in high school, going on a church trip to Europe, and convincing my university that an internship in New York City at NBC News should count toward my study abroad credit.

"You should go next year. I think it would be really good for you," Megan told me after she returned.

I wanted to ask, "Why me? Do you think I need this more than other people? That I'm some sort of racist in need of an intervention?" Instead, I nodded as I told her that I would definitely consider it, even as I wondered why I should sign up to sleep on a bus and travel across state lines in search of answers to a problem I didn't understand or even fully see. I would later realize that what had initially felt like a call-out was actually an invitation.

Over the course of the next year, I watched Megan's friend circle diversify beyond our group of girlfriends (sadly, that didn't take much—as I look back at pictures from college, not only were we all White, but most of us were Swedish and blond), and I saw her engage in new causes and advocacy with the Black Student Association on campus. Something had shifted in her as a result of that trip.

I was drawn to this change, to her sense of purpose, to the stretching and widening I was witnessing. I had always been an idealist. From a young age, I learned about problems or injustices and felt a personal responsibility to make them better. I remember spending many childhood hours poring over a book called *It's Our World Too*. It was filled with stories of kids from all over the country fighting hunger, or raising awareness about AIDS, or standing up to gangs. It inspired me with possibility. It also felt worlds away from where I was growing up.

My childhood years were spent outside of Chicago as the middle child of three to my parents, who had made their way to the northwestern suburbs by way of Iowa. They met on a blind date at Iowa State in the 1960s: my father, the sweet and nerdy English major with his love of words and story and knowledge, and my mother, the whip-smart education major who came from a long line of independent and accomplished women. Despite the disappointment of infertility, they started our family through the adoption of my older sister. Ten years later, my mom was five months pregnant with me before she learned that—miracle of miracles—she was expecting. A few years later after another unexpected but wanted pregnancy for my mom, my younger brother was born.

As we grew up and learned about my sister's adoption story, the details were almost always told the same way: "We didn't even think adoption would be available to us. Our close friends were actually supposed to adopt your sister, but they got pregnant and asked us," Mom would always begin. "I remember getting the call that they had chosen us, hanging up the phone, and literally jumping up and down on our couch. We were so excited," Dad would continue.

The fact that my sister's adoption came through so easily felt like a miracle to my mom and dad. "To adopt a healthy White infant in the United States in the early 1970s was almost impossible, and you would likely be waiting for years," they would often say. But it wasn't just the excitement of a baby coming to our family; it was the marvel that it was a healthy *White* baby. There was no reason stated why a White baby was preferred, but their enthusiasm made it clear.

I can count on one hand the times I remember my family talking about race growing up. This story about my sister's adoption was so ingrained in our family's story that it was years before I recognized it as my first conscious racialized experience. It was the first time skin color had been assigned unequal value, and the first time a hole was poked in the philosophy of sameness and colorblind thinking I was steeped in. I don't believe my parents intended to uphold some sort of White supremacy thinking. But in some ways, it was understood that a White baby would be "easier," partially because it would be less likely to invite complicated questions about our family. Not until many years later did I realize that maybe my parents didn't feel prepared to raise a Black child, or that the "solution" might not have been as simple as White parents adopting kids of color.

But while I learned the words to the song "Jesus Loves the Little Children" and sang earnestly that all the children of the world were indeed precious in his sight, I had this very unexplored experience that led me to wonder if some were more "precious" than others.

●   ●   ●

By the time I turned eleven, I had my Saturday morning TV-watching routine down. I usually had the whole basement to myself, but this Saturday my dad was downstairs working on his computer. That week's episode of the teenage sitcom *California Dreams* was called "Guess Who's Coming to Brunch," and it was more hard-hitting than the show's usual formula of a high school rock band. Tony, the Black drummer, started dating a rich White girl named Kimberly—but when Tony went to meet her parents, Kimberly's dad handed him a check for one thousand dollars to stop dating her.

Kimberly's dad: It just doesn't work. You're both from different worlds.

Tony: Different worlds. You mean because I'm Black?

In the next scene, Tony sits with his all-White bandmates.

Tony's friend: I can't believe he actually asked you not to date Kimberly because you're Black! What did you do?

Tony: What do you think I did? I told him to forget it. It's not like I never met prejudiced people, it's just that the dude seemed so cool.

Jenny's dad (Mr. Garrison) walks into the room, having clearly overheard their conversation: Well, don't be surprised, Tony. A lot of people pretend to be open-minded until they have to deal with someone who's different.

Tony: What about you, Mr. Garrison? Would you have a problem if I started dating Jenny?

Jenny's dad: Of course not.

At this point I looked up from the worn loveseat and caught my dad's eye. I couldn't tell if he had been listening.

As my dad wrapped up his work at the computer, I asked if he had heard any of the episode. He hadn't, so I filled him in, watching his face more intently as I got closer to the crucial, revealing question that would tell me if my dad was like Jenny's dad or Kimberly's dad.

"Would you have a problem if I dated a Black guy, Dad?"

"No," Dad replied. Immediate relief washed over me. My dad passed the test!

And then he continued, "I would just be concerned that if you got married and had kids, it would be hard on them. Mixed race kids often don't know where they belong, and that can be really confusing."

Now I was the one confused. First of all, I was eleven, so even talking hypothetically about dating felt like a stretch, but hypothetical marriage and hypothetical biracial kids? I was not expecting this. More importantly, I still didn't understand my dad's concern, and I walked away from the conversation feeling unclear.

● ● ●

As I look back now, there were other elements of my childhood environment that were puzzling, disparities I noticed about the demographics of my elementary school (the buses that went to single-family houses contained all White kids, while the students who walked to the nearby apartment complex were mostly Black and Brown) and the neighborhood we lived in. But *thankfully*, much of what confused me or made me feel uncomfortable while I was growing up I was merely a witness to, not an active participant. At least that's what I thought. Then one day I found the finger I had been unconsciously pointing at others staring me right in the face.

I worked at Old Navy over winter break of my sophomore year in college. For those four weeks I folded clothes, attended the dressing rooms where I answered questions about fit and whether or not these jeans came in another size, and listened to holiday remixes of all the classics.

It was company policy for employees on the floor to wear headsets. Mine always got too close to my mouth and I almost never had to say anything, so I often wore it with the mic adjusted away from my face, wrapped into the headset band like a headband. It was mostly quiet, but managers would get on to let us know if someone needed to take a break or if there was a line in the dressing room.

Then one afternoon, a shift manager got on and asked me to meet her in the baby section. I adjusted my headset, pushed the "talk" button, and indicated that I was on my way. She was in my ear again before I reached her, her voice lowered to almost a whisper. "There's a family that has been stealing from our store and they are back. I need your help."

"Okay, so do you want me to talk to them or . . ." I started to reply. I could feel my cheeks getting warm and my words trailing off. I was confused as to why she was asking for my help and unsure what to do. At my interview they had only asked about coworkers stealing; they hadn't trained us on how to deal with shoplifters.

"No." The urgency in her voice snapped me back to the moment, to the task at hand. "Just follow my lead and help me catch them."

We left the baby section and turned the corner into the girls section. My manager and I started making our way toward the pair. When I saw the direction she was headed and who was at the center of her search, two Black women came into focus. I couldn't tell how old they were or what they were wearing, but I can tell you that they picked up their pace as we came toward them. And then they made a dash for the exit. I heard my manager shout something that made me instinctively pick up my walk to a jog, and I felt my body carry me out the door after them. I watched them race to their car in the suburban shopping center, clearly empty-handed. And as I slowly walked back into the store, my manager's face showed she was irritated.

"What happened?" she asked.

"Nothing. They got in their car and drove away," I replied as I felt the adrenaline leaving my body and became aware that I had just run outside in December wearing nothing but a thin cotton T-shirt. I realized that I'd just blindly followed my manager and that maybe it wasn't "nothing" that had just happened. Because I couldn't know for sure if I would have chased them if they had been White.

● ● ●

A year later when the Sankofa trip dates were announced and the process opened up, I felt an urgency in my spirit as I turned in my application. For the first time I was starting to be aware of patterns and themes in what I understood before as a smattering of isolated incidents. I wanted to push past a minimal examination that had mostly satisfied me until this point.

When asked in my interview why I wanted to go, I took a few moments, my heart racing and all of these memories whirling as I struggled to form the right response. After what felt like a tad too long to process what should be a simple and obvious question, I heard myself say something about smiling at Black people.

They accepted me on the trip despite my answer. Or more likely because of it.

I cringe at that answer now. And I also still understand it—genuinely feeling the need to be extra friendly in public, to reassure Black strangers on the sidewalk that I wasn't the type of White person they had to worry about (clearly, I had stuffed some of my earlier behavior way down). For most of my life up to my Sankofa interview, the beginning and the end of my thoughts and actions regarding race was: *What should I do to let people know I'm not a racist? Because we all know being racist is really bad. And super mean. So to not be racist probably means to be nice. Smiling is nice. I'll do that. It's such a bummer that African Americans are incarcerated at five times the rate of White people. I've decided the best course of action against this injustice is to smile. Have a great day!*

But here's what I didn't know at the time: that this trip and this antiracism work wasn't reserved for a certain type of White person. It didn't care if I smiled or if I frowned, if I was as nice or as mean as can be. I would come to learn it did not discriminate.

There is nothing wrong with smiling or being nice. The problem is when that becomes the test for how one might actually be complicit in racism. And if as White people our main objective in entering into activism or conversations about race is to prove that because of x, y, or z we couldn't possibly be a racist, we are missing the point. And perhaps, even more importantly, we are missing out.

I most certainly was.

2

DOING NOTHING IS NO LONGER AN OPTION

We've got to get on the same page before we can turn it. . . .
It's time to tell the truth . . . so that we can move forward
with a new story, together.

HEATHER McGHEE

EVERY WEDNESDAY NIGHT FOR THE MONTH leading up to the Sankofa trip, forty students and I crammed inside a small university classroom. Dr. S., one of the Africana studies and sociology professors, created a concentrated course for us, ensuring that we would board that bus with a shared, deeper understanding of both American and world history. A petite, light-skinned Black man with wireframe glasses, an aged, brown leather bag strapped sideways across his chest, and the perfect "I could have had a cameo on *The Cosby Show* as one of the academic friends who rocks a great patterned sweater and traditional kufi hat" professor vibe, Dr. S. was a legend, clearly respected in the academic setting, and relevant, often dropping pop culture movie and music references with ease. He was our guide to the past and present, brilliantly weaving complex themes and nuanced insights from the beginning of humanity to today.

I have known few people in my life living more from the center of who they are than Dr. S. He possessed so many makings of a living legend.

He created a learning environment with so many "Aha" and "Oh no" and "How come no one ever taught me this before now?" moments during almost every class. One of these occurred when he pulled out a world map and pointed to Africa as the origins for the very first humans. He told us we could all trace our DNA back to this continent. *How had I not known this before?* I thought as I stared at the map. He never mocked or shamed or made anyone feel stupid for not knowing. Instead, with a gentle demeanor and firm resolve against injustice and anti-Blackness, he believed deeply in the power of education, of knowing, and of being tethered to the truth in the fight for justice.

Dr. S. called everyone in his class "brother" or "sister" followed by their first name, as in, "There is no race but the human race, Brother John. Race is simply an invented construct of society." And he spoke with a gentleness and conviction woven so tightly together that his words came out emphasized and annunciated and slow, warm, and soft all at once. It was a consistent voice. One that asked questions. One that drew questions and curiosity out of us.

When we examined the writers of the Constitution, Dr. S. would poke at the signers, saying, "Forefathers—whose fathers? These are not my fathers." And as he taught through the lyrics to the rap song "F*** Tha Police" by N.W.A., he rapped along with the chorus of the track, trading the cuss word for the letter *f*. Hearing him softly chant, "Eff the police," we sensed his deep anger toward an institution that arrested and killed Black men at a disproportionate rate.

As I've told many others who are encountering more accurate history for the first time, it's like learning a new language with new terms and definitions. But it was much bigger than that because it was also a thesis that challenged the one I had been told my whole life. Many of the other White students and I were starting to understand this lexicon more quickly than we felt comfortable speaking it. Dr. S. was patient with us as we nervously and quietly began to ask questions, our voices trying out new words and our minds trying out new ideas. "How is my view of the world not only *not* colorblind, but incredibly racialized?" a

White student asked one evening. In response, we were invited to examine what we had been taught as objectives in our history books. Dr. S. taught and brought alive terms like *Eurocentric* (which gave language as to why my education around the world often felt narrow and one-sided) and *Afrocentric* in hopes that by recognizing the lens with which we saw the world, we would also embrace his invitation for our view to be expanded.

But he wasn't just offering us different lenses or a taste of critical thinking; he was modeling his own vision *for* the world, one where he sat with the Black students in the campus cafeteria instead of mingling with the other professors, and encouraged his White students to question everything, especially the things that appeared to benefit us. He cracked me open to help me understand and believe stories that were different from the ones I had heard and digested with ease, without a second thought, my whole life.

At the end of our last class with Dr. S., trip partners were announced—each Black student paired with a non-Black student. When I heard "Jenny and . . . Katrina," I found Katrina's face across the room. We both smiled apprehensively. Katrina and I knew of each other more than we knew each other, and as they read the remaining names, I searched my memories for ones that included her.

I could locate only one—a college basketball game. I had sat in the stands as I watched the cheerleaders in their gold and blue uniforms run across the glossy gym floor and begin their cheer. They were all White. All except one. As I watched the lone Black girl stand with the others and clap and cheer and kick and shout, I was struck not only because she was the only Black girl but also because she looked like a Disney princess. Katrina's hair was pulled back into a high ponytail, curled at the ends. Her smile was bright and warm, and she moved to the beat of the crowd's clapping with an assurance that looked confident, not cocky or cheesy.

Back in the classroom, we waited until the last names were called before we left our desks and made our way toward each other. Katrina formally introduced herself and then quickly added, "But we already know each other, right?"

"I think so," I said with a bit of nervous, excited laughter in my voice. There was a row of desks between us, which felt symbolic. "They recommend getting to know each other better before we leave for the trip. Do you want to get coffee sometime?"

"Sure. Sounds good." She gave me the same warm smile I remembered from her courtside cheer.

A few days later, when we met at the coffee shop in the basement of one of the university dorms, we quickly made the connection that Katrina grew up in a suburb about thirty minutes away from my hometown with her parents and two brothers. She was her high school's prom queen and a cheerleader, and now an honor roll student at our college, majoring in communications.

"I'm pretty used to being 'the only one' in most spaces I occupy," Katrina said. "Growing up, I was almost always the only Black girl, and usually the only Black person in my classes. Even here with the courses I'm taking I am always the exception, never the standard. You would think I would be used to it by now, which I sort of am. It helps that there are more Black people here than there were back home."

"Yeah, that makes so much sense." I racked my brain for times when I had been "the only one." The few memories that came were fleeting, not representing an entire lifetime full of onliness. I had been the only girl many times, but I couldn't remember ever being the only White person in a space.

Katrina continued telling me another story about growing up being the only Black girl. Her story mirrored my own memories of sleepovers in elementary school almost exactly, right down to the Paula Abdul dances. Until it didn't.

When I was in second grade, I went to a sleepover at a friend of a friend's house. I was so excited to finally be old enough to go to one—it felt like a rite of passage. We were having so much fun listening to Mariah Carey and Paula Abdul and making up choreographed dances.

Then, when it was time for us to go to sleep, I pulled out my sleeping bag. I still remember it was pink, covered in characters from Strawberry Shortcake. I put my sleeping bag on the floor between the girl hosting and the friend who invited me. The girl who was hosting looked at me and said aloud, "You can't sleep next to me." The room fell silent, and in that moment, my feelings were only a little hurt and I trembled out a feeble "Why?" as I racked my second-grade brain trying to figure out what I'd done wrong to offend her so deeply that even my sleeping bag being next to hers was now a night-changing trigger. We'd had so much fun I couldn't imagine what I could have done.

"Because Black people have bugs."

Katrina's voice rose as she continued to imitate that little White girl, probably seven or eight years old: "*Black* people have bugs in their hair because they're dirty!" As Katrina's face contorted from her impersonation, she still wore a look of pain. "I knew I was not dirty. I knew there were no bugs in my hair. But at that moment I felt dirty. I looked at the girls around the room. I looked at my friend who invited me."

Katrina shared that instead of showing any signs of distrust toward that bold, false proclamation, all the White girls looked as if they'd learned something new about Black people that night—as if they'd heard a truth that they could now begin to apply to their lives. Katrina had looked around the room. It was quiet for a few seconds. Then, total eruption: shrieks of "Eww" and "Gross" or "Don't sleep next to me, either!" or "Black people have bugs!"

"For the first time in my life, I became aware of myself. I became aware of my hair," Katrina said. "I think I was really shaken to the core by how easily all the White girls trusted this one White girl's lie. It was as if they'd never known me. It was as if we hadn't just spent the entire evening playing, giggling, dancing, singing, being silly, and sharing snacks together. I didn't have a word for it then, but now I know what I felt. *Disposable.*" Katrina's eyes glistened as she held back tears.

But Katrina didn't cry, even when she told me that the little girl's mom was in the room the whole time. The adult in the room didn't tell the girls to stop. The adult did not correct what they said. The adult didn't make any effort to reassure Katrina. The adult—in the room *the whole time*—heard and saw what happened, and chose to do nothing.

Katrina's tone shifted. She sounded like she was talking to that little Black girl, assuring her she had every right to be angry and hurt by what that moment stole from her. "I had to call my mom to come pick me up. When my mom got there, it was like she knew, like this feeling of being publicly shamed was familiar for her too. She cried when I told her what they had said. I felt robbed of a moment from childhood and I still do, probably always will. This was my very first sleepover."

Katrina went on to explain the significance of that experience. That night she realized that even the people she thought were her friends, and the grownups she thought she could trust, could hurt or humiliate her. That reality was more painful than what was actually said at the sleepover.

That experience was a turning point for her. After that sleepover, Katrina's dad started telling her and her brothers how to protect themselves when around White folks. They were given explicit instructions: their behavior in public was to be exceptional, quiet, respectful, and not too attention-getting. When Katrina's parents had "the talk" with her it wasn't about the birds and the bees like in my house—it was about how to interact with police, how to dress to be seen as "not a threat," and how to put her hands in the air immediately if a cop ever pulled her over whether she was driving or not.

While shopping, her parents told her over and over not to touch anything on the shelves or racks and to avoid putting her hands in her coat pockets or purse. If followed, she should make eye contact and smile to appear friendly. When checking out at a store, she had to keep the receipt in her hand until she left so as not to allow anyone to accuse her of stealing.

The only thing I knew about shopping was a quote from my German great-grandmother my mom liked to reference while we stood in line at the grocery store: "You open de eyes or you open de pocketbook." While I was given instructions on how to minimize an accidental overcharge, Katrina and her brothers were given instruction on how to avoid being falsely accused or even killed.

"Why did you want to go on Sankofa?" she asked, turning the focus to me.

I started to pull out my rehearsed answer but paused. Just from the last few hours I realized how much I didn't know, like I'd only had half the story, but without knowing how much I was missing. "I think so we could have this conversation. And hopefully more conversations like this. There is so much I don't know but that I really want to understand." After a brief pause, I returned the favor. "Why did *you* want to go on Sankofa?"

"I didn't."

I was definitely not expecting that. I held my breath and held her gaze as I waited for her to continue.

"I went last year and my partner was a girl from Kansas, and we had an awful experience together," said Katrina. "After we went to a planta-tion, she started crying. When I asked her what she was thinking, she told me she was sad about being sad and that she didn't like that feeling. Nothing about sadness over the history or the evil of owning other humans. Sad about feeling sad. What a waste of a weekend, of my time and energy. A few months ago, the leaders of the trip basically begged me to come back because they didn't have enough Black students."

I would learn later that the White students had to apply to be accepted on the trip because so many of us were interested in going, while the Black students were essentially recruited, and most went more than once. (I chalked that up to the ratio of White to Black students. Now I'm pretty sure that wasn't the only reason. The ratio wasn't just about numbers; this took less out of the White students and required more from the Black students.)

"But I think this year might be different."

I exhaled audibly. *I sure hope so*, I thought.

I didn't know how to feel as I packed my bag the night before Sankofa. But I knew I was ready to listen and open to hearing more. And I would try to quiet any belief that because Katrina and I had some things in common it meant we were coming from the exact same place.

● ● ●

We left Chicago early Friday morning. Katrina and I found seats near the back of the bus while our university's leaders, a White man in his twenties and a Black woman in her thirties, gave instructions over the microphone at the front of the bus. None of the students knew where we were headed, since the trip never went the same route and the leaders purposely kept the itinerary from us.

Aside from a trip to Florida, I had never been to the South before. I couldn't tell any difference from the highway but for the power of the sun. Our group was quite the sight at the first rest stop: a perfect ratio of Black and White students tumbling off the bus and into the lines for bathrooms and food. I pictured the Freedom Riders that Dr. S. had taught us about—the group of over four hundred civil rights activists who started riding buses in 1961 into the segregated South to challenge local segregated seating laws. Though many were teenagers and young adults, they were a crucial part of the civil rights movement. When Dr. S. taught, he had displayed a dozen or so mug shots: several Black men and women, a handful of White men, and a few White women.

I wondered if anybody watching us at the rest stop thought about the Freedom Riders too. Because in that moment I realized that we could not have made this trip if the Freedom Riders and many others quite literally hadn't paved the way. I flashed back to another image Dr. S. had shared, one of a bus set on fire by a White mob in Anniston, Alabama, a huge cloud of smoke billowing into the air. As I looked out my bus's smoke-free, un-smashed windows, I felt the extra weight of an invitation to learn not only about the awful history of White supremacy but also about those who had fought against racism along the way.

● ● ●

The significance of those first two days couldn't be overstated. Our group visited three different sites that each prompted new questions and, honestly, a lot of discomfort.

Our first stop was the John Perkins's Center in Jackson, Mississippi. The founder, Dr. John Perkins, was a community developer, author, and minister who had experienced much racism and hatred in his lifetime. We learned Dr. Perkins lost his brother, Clyde, a World War II veteran and recipient of a Purple Heart, to police violence when John was only seventeen. John himself was beaten and tortured while in jail after participating in a protest at the age of forty, but he "hadn't let it make [him] bitter." He started the center to meet both the physical and spiritual needs of the community.

I was inspired. Here was someone doing something in the face of all these wrongs. Maybe the trip leaders brought our group here to show us examples of what we could do once we graduated.

The conversation started to shift when we found out the Black man hosting us was a newlywed married to a White woman. I noticed a change in demeanor among some of the students. A few Black girls shared about the pain of seeing Black men with non-Black women—how it felt like betrayal, a passing over. How finding a non-Black partner could be seen as climbing an invisible social hierarchy, with Black women at the bottom and White women at the top. Some girls named couples who exhibited the dynamic of a Black man with a non-Black woman: celebrities and leaders and professors and pastors.

I recognized that this was not the time to ask if anyone had ever seen that one episode of *California Dreams*. The conclusion I had made as a child based on one episode of Saturday morning TV—that being con-flicted in regard to interracial relationships was objectively racist—was incredibly simplistic. As I listened, I realized that I had nothing to add to a conversation as nuanced as this one.

As people continued to process and share, I recognized that the hypo-thetical union with a Black man I had asked my dad about might not be received as progress, as the ushering in of an open-minded, colorblind, and tolerant world, but instead for some it would simply be another layer of pain to process and grieve.

While I had one wobbly frame of reference to pull from, many of the Black students around me were standing atop a foundation constructed painfully over multiple generations and countless moments. A founda-tion filled with the knowledge of a long lineage of enslaved Black women consistently, repeatedly, and strategically raped with no consequence to the attacker. A foundation filled with accounts of mobs and murder to punish Black men accused of looking at, talking to, or walking too close to White women. A foundation filled with the clear commonality of White women being "protected" and Black women being preyed on.

No one in that room was saying that interracial relationships should never happen or were racist, but that wasn't the point. The point was that there was pain in that room, and it wouldn't just go away without, at the very least, being named and acknowledged. I walked back onto the bus, confronted again that my understanding of the past made it a lot harder to truly see and understand the present—that so much of what I had learned or witnessed growing up had been missing important historical context. Suddenly the meaning of the trip—looking back in order to move forward—started to click. These few moments from the first day left me hungry for more.

● ● ●

The next morning, the bus pulled up to our second location. If I squinted, I could see acres of fields and a few large old farm buildings with worn gray wood on the sides. Large trees that looked a thousand years old adorned the entrance to the Frogmore Cotton Plantation, while the fresh, sweet scent of flowers wafted into the dry air. Off in the distance were several smaller cabin-like buildings with worn white siding and red roofs. I watched a group of elementary school students being led on a tour of their own, mostly White students with a few Black children as well.

A White woman appeared in front of our group wearing period attire: a large white blouse and a pale red cotton skirt. After greeting us with a Southern drawl that matched her ensemble, she quickly split our group in two.

Katrina and I were in the first group, and the tour started with the slaves' quarters. We took turns stepping into the tight room, taking it all in quickly so as to give everyone a chance to see. The room was unimpressive, with worn, exposed wood on the floors, walls, and ceiling. Thin fabric hung over the only window as a makeshift curtain. There was a single bed frame with a lumpy looking "mattress." Our guide pointed out that not all slave quarters were "this nice"—the difference was because these owners "treated their slaves well."

Next, we squeezed our way through the doors of the church, a larger building with the original exterior but with what appeared to be new wood floors, new large windows, and eight rows of wooden benches along each side of the aisle. We sat on the benches as a TV was wheeled in to show us a bit about "what life was like back then."

As we watched, we heard the voice of an older Southern man. He spoke of the family that lived there having a deep desire to share their Christian faith with the slaves. They had built the church as a place to express their faith. Everyone looked forward to Sundays, as it was a day of rest meant to worship God. Songs and music were incredibly important in the work structure and social lives of the people on plantations.

At this, the chorus of an African American spiritual filled the room. We heard lyrics of longing—promises that those enslaved would not be here for much longer.

Through those TV speakers, I felt the beauty, hope, and sadness that music so powerfully offers. I sat in the room where some of these songs possibly originated, looking out through the windows at the view that those singing not so many years ago had also seen. It occurred to me that this church had not just been built *for* the enslaved but *by* them as well. This was a place intent on holding Black bodies and souls captive to the needs of the White owners.

"Does anyone have any questions so far?" Our guide's voice broke into the moment.

"Did anyone try to escape? Try to head north and become free?" a Black student asked.

"No. For a few reasons—the first being that the grounds were surrounded by swampy, unsafe conditions and dangerous wildlife. And the second, they were actually treated relatively well here because they had good owners."

"How can anyone owning another human be good?" This same student spoke again, his voice indicating that he was making a statement more than asking a question.

The guide explained that the housing and opportunities for the slaves on that plantation were good for the times and "compared to other plantations in the area," where many other masters and mistresses provided "next to nothing." She responded matter-of-factly, but her tone was too light, as if the weight of these questions could just be blown away and dismissed if needed.

"What about compared to where the enslaver and his family lived? How did that compare?" another Black student added.

The guide continued to appear unbothered, albeit frustrated that her point wasn't being understood and that the students kept asking the same questions in different ways.

We saw the next group outside waiting for us to finish so we could switch. Our guide looked relieved at the interruption and distraction from the questions she refused to answer, and quickly ushered us out of the church building toward a giant field. Rows and rows of brown twigs covered with bright white cotton balls were laid out before us up to the horizon line. It was oddly beautiful, like a snowscape in the middle of a warm, sunny Southern day.

And then our guide made a stunning final remark. "Before you all leave, you are welcome to pick cotton from this field. We have these historical sacks for anyone who would like to try it. It's actually a very fun and popular activity here."

We all just stood there for a moment. Had she really just suggested that pretending to be an enslaved person picking cotton would be fun? After a brief, shocked silence from our group, there were shouts of "This is so messed up," and "Today has been filled with lies," and "Haven't you already had enough Black people pick your cotton for free?" Apparently, this was the last straw for our guide. I saw her motion to our trip leaders and heard her not so discreetly use words like "disrespected" and "out of line."

The tour was over, but as we got back on the bus, the emotions it dug up were not. Katrina seemed really upset, and we sat in silence for a while. Katrina finally broke the silence. "You are able to walk into a space like that and automatically trust what's being said," she said after a few minutes. I could tell that *you* wasn't meant just for me; it was for all White people—on and off the bus.

I imagined our White guide as a young girl on the same tour as the one she had just led, hearing about the "good slave owners" and "respect for one's culture and pride in their Southern history." I imagined her hearing those messages over and over throughout the years from people she loved and trusted.

Was this woman so different from me? Every story I'd heard had taught me to trust the White voice, defend the White perspective, defer to the White expert. What we had just experienced wasn't designed for Katrina or any other Black person who walked those grounds. It was for White people like me. I wondered how I could learn to see the world on someone else's terms when the learning curve felt so steep.

• • •

At the third stop, our bus pulled through a large collegiate-looking iron gate as our leaders disclosed that we had arrived at a lynching exhibition. We stepped inside and immediately were faced with a giant quilted map of the United States that covered the entire wall of the room. My eyes were immediately drawn to the Midwest—Illinois, Iowa, Minnesota, Indiana, and Michigan—muscle memory from years of looking at maps in class and always viewing the world from where I came from. The map had a marking for every location a confirmed lynching had occurred. The markings were all over, more prevalent in the Southern states but not at all absent from the North. There was no clear divide between the Union and the Confederate, the "good guys" I learned about in fifth grade who fought selflessly to free the enslaved, and the "bad guys" who delighted in owning human beings.

To the right of the map was a box listing the names of people who had been lynched and the years. I blinked again and again as I scanned the dates, as if blinking enough times would cause the information to make sense. The first several numbers computed—all in the late 1700s through mid-1900s—until I saw 1971, 1979, 1982, 1987, 1992, 1994. My eyes hung on 1982. I was born in 1982.

Silently I continued to the next room and over to one of the clear display cases filled with old newspaper clippings. I scanned headline after headline, all reporting on lynchings.

LYNCHED: Alfred Blount, a Negro, Suffers Death

THE HIDEOUS CRIME: Mrs. Moore, mother of four children, was brutally attacked at her home in the city.

AND THE PENALTY DEATH: A thousand men surround the jail after night, one hundred force an entrance and secure their prey.

I forced my legs to carry me to the next display case filled with photographs and postcards. In one photograph, crowds of hundreds of White people of all ages grinned and pointed in the foreground while a

Black body hung lifeless in the background. In their non-pointing hands, the White people held "souvenirs" of cut-up parts of the body they had just watched be killed.

I felt sick.

Everything was abhorrent, but the fact that whole families showed up to watch someone be brutally murdered was the most upsetting and shocking observation. Looking into the eyes of White children at these lynchings and observing the ease of their smiles, without a hint of shame or conflicting feelings, was like seeing a visual baton of hatred passed from one generation to the next. In her Pulitzer Prize–winning book *The Warmth of Other Suns* about the Great Migration, Isabel Wilkerson recaps such a scene.

> Fifteen thousand men, women, and children gathered to watch eighteen-year-old Jesse Washington as he was burned alive in Waco, Texas, in May 1916. The crowd chanted, "Burn, burn, burn!" as Washington was lowered into the flames. One father holding his son on his shoulders wanted to make sure his toddler saw it. "My son can't learn too young," the father said.

If hatred is taught, these kids were learning as young as possible. Their parents and their communities were making sure of it.

Suddenly, the silence of our group was shattered by a guttural scream. My head snapped in that direction, finding Michelle, a Black student in our group. Members of our group gathered around and helped her exit the room. The rest of our group quickly followed, unsure of what had just happened.

"She recognized a family name in one of the articles she saw in there," said one Black student. "The name of a man who had been lynched. It's so awful. Man. I was terrified I would see one of my relatives too."

"Didn't we, though?" another Black student added.

My body kept moving, but my mind played those words over and over. *"Didn't we, though?"* When I was scanning the faces of those smiling back at me in the pictures, I wasn't thinking about how I was connected to them. I didn't think to check the names out of fear that one would match my own, confirming that lynching was part of my family's personal history. Instead, I engaged (as I thought one does) with a history lesson about something that happened "a very long time ago" or a news program about something "way over there." How was that possible, and what allowed me this disconnection? Perhaps it was the "I wouldn't have been there" and "I'm not like *those* White people" rationale I had often believed about myself. But in that moment, I started to wonder how I had always been so sure of myself.

Back on the bus, the mood was somber. I wasn't sure everyone had heard about Michelle, but our leaders stood at the front of the bus and encouraged us to come forward and process what we'd just experienced. At some point, a White girl started talking in the microphone. She looked out at us and stumbled her way through something about how families had suffered during the Holocaust. Then her voice gained more confidence as she declared it wasn't only about hatred between "Blacks and Whites" and there was danger of a victim mentality at stake—that maybe some of us really needed to get more familiar with history because oppression was not something that White people invented. "Look at the Bible! There are slaves in there that weren't owned by White people," she said. I imagined she wanted to put air quotes around the word "White" the way she emphasized it.

A Black student responded by sharing how painful it was to see what she just saw in the museum and then to hear what she just heard on the bus. "Maybe White folks are just inherently evil. Maybe it's not their fault. Maybe they truly don't know any other way of existing besides stealing and greed and violence and the continued dehumanization of others." She said it so calmly you would have thought she was telling you what she had for breakfast that day. She spoke of deep pain, but there was not a hint of surprise in her voice.

There was some applause as she put the microphone back in its stand. I could feel Katrina's eyes on me. Our bus had a section of seats that faced each other, so while most everyone else sat side-by-side with their partner, Katrina and I were face-to-face. Eye-to-eye.

Her wide brown eyes looked into mine, and for a few moments we just sat there, silent, eyes locked. The intimacy of the moment was surprising, and maybe because we were surrounded by discomfort, the normal temptation to look away wasn't there.

Watching Katrina's face as each excuse was made changed how I heard those comments. What I might have previously accepted as understandable or even logical claims became much harder to tolerate as I watched her react.

More students got up, and the game of verbal ping-pong continued: "White people on the bus, feel the pain of racism and all that we are holding, please . . ." *Whack.* "I just don't like being held responsible for something when I wasn't even alive . . ." *Whack.* "This was supposed to be about opening up minds . . ." *Whack.* "I didn't even know, and now you are trying to make me feel guilty. . . ."

Katrina let out an audible sigh. And then she slowly mouthed the words, "Jenny, go say something." I'm not sure she knew what was going to happen next, but I know I needed that push, that permission. Without it I don't know if I would have embraced that moment. Her words propelled my body forward as I walked down the bus aisle. I grabbed the microphone and turned to what felt like a crowd that had doubled in size.

"I'm not sure what to say," I started. "I'm obviously White, so I have to imagine today has felt different for me than for many of you. As I've listened to other people speak from this microphone, I feel like there is a finite amount of empathy and understanding that is on display, and it's being rationed out across every injustice as opposed to being added to it." I imagined the White students trying to spread out a pile of salt, one pinch at a time. "Slavery gets a teeny tiny pinch. Lynching gets a wee bit. The Holocaust another sprinkle."

I was trying to express that maybe we didn't have to talk about *everything* horrible in history, or justify and make excuses, distancing ourselves from the history and experiences we were there to focus on. I felt completely out of my body and in my head, not sure if this was making any sense or helping at all. And then I heard applause. When I realized that it came from several Black students, something deep inside me broke. My soul didn't just crack open. It exploded. I knew I didn't deserve this display of grace, so I began to cry.

I forced myself to look into the faces of those grace givers. They could have easily, without justification or a second thought, said, "Thanks but no thanks. Your little speech was too little and way too late." But their response moved me even more than what I had seen within the walls of the lynching museum or heard from the plantation tour. It felt like an invitation to change, or hopefully confirmation that I was already starting to.

The tears didn't stop, and neither did my words.

"I can't fix your pain, but I can see it. And I will work for the rest of my life so that your children don't experience the pains of racism the same ways you have." And then I said nine words that I have never forgotten: "Doing nothing is no longer an option for me."

I put the microphone back in its stand and started to make my way down the aisle of the bus when a Black girl pulled me into an empty seat next to her. Her eyes were tender and moist. "Jenny, when you were standing up there, your mascara was running, and your tears turned black. When you were giving in to the pain, instead of avoiding it, something changed. And not just for you. But for a lot of us."

It took me a minute to truly understand what that meant. "My name is Austin," she said next. I couldn't know it then, but the path of my life had just shifted. There was no going back, only "looking back in order to keep moving forward." *Sankofa* indeed.

3

"OMG KAREN, YOU CAN'T JUST ASK PEOPLE WHY THEY'RE WHITE"

MEAN *GIRLS* THE MOVIE

Here's one delusion: that we can escape slavery.
We can't. Its scars will never fade.

COLSON WHITEHEAD

"JENNY, HOW WAS SANKOFA?" people would ask casually upon my return. Every time I would freeze up for a second, then say a few vague sentences and try to move the conversation along. I was not surprised by their asking. Our college was relatively small and the trip was well-known. In their curiosity I realized quickly how protective I was of the experience, and especially that moment when I spoke. It felt so intimate, so powerful and transformative, and maybe even a little like returning from a holy space. I wanted to talk about it with friends, but I worried that in the wrong hands it might feel cheap or unimportant. I didn't want anything tainting my memory of such a life-altering, significant moment. More importantly, I didn't want anything to slow me down as I continued my journey.

I was still processing what had shifted in me, and I was concerned that sharing with most White people would make me feel defensive or like I was trying to convince them of something. So I wanted to share with one of the few people I had already talked to about race before I left. I started with my friend Angie, who is Mexican and White. It went really well; she asked good questions and stayed engaged throughout. So I reached out to a few White friends to set up coffee dates, where they mostly listened and reflected back that it sounded like a really meaningful trip. I was relieved.

I had let my guard down a bit when I shared with a friend who very quickly pushed back. "I totally get that for you, with a family that has been in the United States for hundreds of years, you might feel guilty or responsible or something," she said. She continued, "But I don't think everyone needs to feel that way. My grandparents and great-grandparents were still in Sweden back when all this was going on, so I really don't see what this has to do with me. It's not my fault that Black people in the United States were treated this way."

I tried to respond, to help her see that not only was "back then, when all this was really going on," also occurring today, but that anyone White like us benefited from the racist ways systems and structures operated—no matter when our ancestors arrived. We went back and forth in arguments a few times until she got up and walked out of my apartment.

After my friend left, I did a quick search about whether Sweden had been involved in the slave trade. It was. In fact, a longer history of the slave trade existed than I realized. First, Sweden enslaved people from the British Isles, Ireland, and Eastern Europe. This practice lasted from the sixth through eleventh centuries until it was formally abolished in 1335. Then Sweden became part of the transatlantic slave trade, shipping and trading Africans (particularly Ghanaians) from 1650 until 1847, when it became one of the last countries in Europe to end slavery. Also, it was a major supplier of the iron chains used in the slave trade.

I assume my friend didn't know this information either. And even if I had known all of this, I'm not sure that presenting the facts that dispelled her logic would have changed anything. She used her confident ignorance to avoid and deflect just like I had seen other White students do. Just like I had done. I was starting to recognize a pattern of White people's defensiveness, thinking our lack of direct involvement in the past canceled out any responsibility for the present. And I was starting to realize this didn't just happen on a trip like Sankofa when emotions were running high. When it came to the issue of racism, it happened all the time.

I was becoming more familiar with naming this reaction for what it was—a need to create distance between the problem and oneself. But we weren't just discussing some abstract *problem*; we were talking about *people*.

All that year, our university campus had been asking the question, "Who is my neighbor?" We were looking to the passage in Luke where a teacher of the law, knowing the command to love our neighbor, asked Jesus that same question. Jesus responded with the story of a man beaten and left for dead at the side of the road. Two people—religious leaders—passed by before a third stopped to help. That third person did not stop because he was responsible for the state of the man or because he was related to the injured. And he didn't stop because he was the same ethnicity or religion. He stopped because he was loving his neighbor. Wasn't Katrina our neighbor? Austin? The other students we had classes with? Jesus' command to love did not hinge on whether we were responsible for any pain in our neighbors' lives.

A full year after I said those words at the front of that bus—that doing nothing was no longer an option for me—my life looked very different as a result.

My relationships with Katrina and Austin and other students were growing as we worked together on our school's chapter of the National Association for the Advancement of Colored People (NAACP). Many of us volunteered with the local coalition for immigrant and refugee rights, and registered people to vote at the nearby "L" station, and attended meetings about making our campus more equitable. But we weren't just working together. We also went shopping together downtown, watched movies in each other's dorm rooms, went out dancing, and raided each other's closets before seeing Lauryn Hill in concert. We were becoming real friends.

I had changed my major and spent a summer interning in New York City for an organization committed to racial and ethnic understanding. I was learning about the many issues on the line when we vote and was determined to vote with these issues (and the people most affected by them) in mind.

My classes on African history messed with the way I saw the world even more. Taught by the brilliant Kenyan professor Theodora Ayot, who wore brightly colored traditional Kenyan dresses and told us stories of "her people," her class helped us see issues and news through a more Afrocentric lens. Each week we were to bring a news article from an African newspaper with a brief summary of the larger issues displayed in that seemingly isolated report. One time I brought in an article about Zimbabwe's new election reforms and was quickly able to trace what was being reported back to the country's relatively recent break from British rule. Professor Ayot was training us to see the unjust patterns of history and their often brutal aftermath, and that very little happens in isolation. The events of the world are often more *reaction* than action. If we wanted to change the effect, we would have to better understand the cause. I was learning about the larger issues and smaller threads that helped racism evolve and adapt. I began to think of myself as a well-meaning ally.

"She gets it now," I overheard one of the trip leaders say the night we got back from Sankofa. I relished the look of approval I got as we stood inside the campus chapel. It was like I was part of the inner circle of White people who could see the world as it truly is, and now I was on the right side of history. I believed people either got it or they didn't. And I pretty much got it. Or at least, I thought I did. Which was why I was so surprised the first time someone didn't quite understand that.

I was in charge of our university's annual arts night, so when I reached out to a Black student who had written and performed a piece of poetry the year before to see if he would share it again, I was slightly taken aback when he responded with a quick and deliberate no. The piece had been about his experience in the world as a Black man, and he had sat at his Djembe drum adding percussion while his White girlfriend read his words of being followed, harassed, mistook, profiled, ignored, and feared. The juxtaposition had been so intentional—his words out of her mouth. I looked at our lineup of performances with several Black and Latinx people sharing and felt determined to convince him that maybe his no was a bit premature, that he might actually feel like he was missing out.

On the phone, I expressed how his poem would fit so beautifully with what others were preparing for the event. I pleaded with him that he didn't have to worry because I "got it" and I was an ally—I assumed that was part of the reason he wasn't saying yes. But he was certain—he didn't want to read his poem again. "It took a lot of energy to share already, and so many students had wanted to talk to me—no, not talk—more like interrogate me as a result," he said. "I don't want to go through explaining and defending my words, my life, ever again. Not if I can help it."

I realized that unless my "getting it" made a difference to him or served him in a way that meant less pain or more safety and joy, it was only really serving me. I was not entitled to his time or anything else I asked for. As a White woman, I owed him the benefit of the doubt, not the other way around.

● ● ●

After graduation, my college boyfriend—a tall, sparkly brown-eyed, dimpled White boy from Minnesota named John—and I both got jobs in Washington, DC. John had been on the Sankofa trip with me and was the coeditor for our college's social justice magazine. Now he worked at a progressive Christian magazine while I worked in fundraising for an educational nonprofit. At first, living in DC felt like looking at the world through pro-Black colored glasses. It's often referred to as "Chocolate City" because of its historic Black roots and the District's demographics.

Coming from a colorblind philosophy, I felt like Dorothy opening the door to a world no longer black and white but full of color. I knew it wasn't perfect, as I walked by neighborhood housing projects filled with a Black majority of residents, yet DC seemed to sparkle with possibility and promise and pride.

Every morning, I left my brick row house and boarded a city bus for the ride to my office. The bus route took me past Malcolm X Park, famous for its history of being ground zero for Black power organizing in the 1960s. The first time I strolled through the park, I heard it before I saw it—the rhythm and steady beats of the drummers gathered for the weekly drum circle, the laughter of small kids as they danced to the beat, the claps and expressions of encouragement from those on the circle's perimeter. The large crowd assembled was often young and old and Black and Brown and White. If one was wearing traditional African kente cloth or had dreadlocks flowing down their back, they wouldn't be the only one.

Next stop on my bus route was Howard University, an HBCU (Historically Black College and University), referred to by many as the "Black Harvard." The alumni list was full of well-known activists, artists, politicians, and prose-makers, including Vice President Kamala Harris, author Toni Morrison, activist and Congressman Andrew Young, and *Top Chef* (personal) favorite Carla Hall. I would see students sporting their Howard tees at neighborhood dance clubs, where we danced alongside each other to live reggae music.

The bus would drive past U Street where the food, music, museums, and history centered on all things Black culture. The birthplace of jazz legend Duke Ellington was one of U Street's favorite bragging rights. My taste buds, my knowledge, and my love of African cuisine expanded exponentially as I tore off spongy injera and scooped up steaming red lentils and collard greens with my hands at one of the many popular and crowded Ethiopian restaurants. Bronze plaques hung outside buildings; a bank cited its significance at being the first African American–owned and run business in the country. The walls of Ben's Chili Bowl were covered from top to bottom with newspaper clippings and signed head-shots from presidents to politicians to musicians to what felt like every great celebrity throughout the years since its opening in 1958.

You could find every type of person in DC. They were my neighbors, my coworkers, the people I attended church with. Coming from the incredibly segregated city of Chicago and its surrounding suburbs, I felt there was real proximity and integration among the people of DC. I felt like I was living much further into a still imperfect but very progressive future.

We lived in this city grateful for its pride in the Black experience and culture. The community I found in DC included people working in non-profits and politics and social justice media, all trying to bring healing and justice to the broken and the unfair.

At least, that's what I thought we were all doing.

● ● ●

In the basement of our office complex was a gym with a few tread-mills, some stationary bikes, and some weights. It wasn't much, but it was free to anyone who worked in the building (and the other twenty-somethings and I would rather spend our gym money on discounted food and drinks at Friday night happy hour). Usually, three or four of us worked out together. Today only Tiffany and I had the time.

Tiffany was our organization's executive assistant working primarily for the executive director. She was petite, blond, preppy, and pretty. A sorority girl from the Eastern Shore of Maryland, she spoke with a slight Southern twang in her vowels, her words often punctuated by a long "o" sound and the snap of gum that she was almost always chewing.

I had just finished my workout while processing the news of a mass shooting at Virginia Tech. The tiny TV mounted in the gym's corner was showing footage of the victims' faces, and I was trying not to cry as I finished my time on the treadmill. As I walked into the locker room, I noticed Tiffany and someone I didn't recognize, a young Black woman from a different company in the building. We showered and changed mostly in silence. As the Black woman left the changing room and we heard the thud of the outer door, Tiffany popped a fresh piece of gum in her mouth and muttered in my direction, "I hate how Black girls' hair smells."

I sat there stunned and, worse, silent. I was confused. We worked with Black women who I assumed Tiffany liked and cared about, yet this was such a mean and racist thing to think, let alone share. She seemed to think this comment would be . . . welcomed? Tolerated? Embraced? Echoed? In that moment, I realized she hadn't said it to the woman who would very likely be offended; she had said it to me because she felt comfortable saying it to another White woman.

Before I could collect myself, Tiffany had left. And I was left with my guilt and my thoughts. I thought of Katrina and the girls making fun of her hair at the sleepover. I thought of Austin putting edge control in her hair before we left for our shopping dates in the city. I thought of the Black women in our office with their box braids and twists. I just hadn't thought of them quickly enough.

It is said that in distressing situations we experience either fight, flight, or freeze. In that moment I froze. Unlike the lengthy Sankofa bus ride, which was also incredibly distressing, this felt like an emotional drive-by. There was a quickness to it that stunned me. I wondered how I would ever be able to get to fight mode when an incident occurred with no warning.

For me (and I think for others), when I realize just how much I don't know and how narrow my scope has been, I tend to run toward others who have had a similar awakening or reorientation of view. It makes so much sense—there is such relief in realizing you are not alone, that you are not the only one with those values or perspectives. Not the only one who sees the world through a similar lens.

I was naive to think that the culture of Black pride in Washington, DC's city streets somehow translated to zero anti-Blackness in the hearts and minds and policies and histories surrounding me. I was projecting my own attitudes about why it was important to work there on everyone else, which was why Tiffany's comment felt particularly shocking. I so desperately wanted to see signs of hope around me that I had excused smaller and less overt racist comments she had made in the past, telling myself I must have misunderstood—until there was no room for misinterpretation.

● ● ●

At church that Sunday, we closed our time together the way we always did: getting out of our folding chairs and making a circle, joining hands, and singing. Our church was tiny, maybe twenty-five people if we were all in attendance. The room was small, so we never felt like we were missing a whole bunch of folks. We sang, "Bind us together, Lord, bind us together with cords that cannot be broken."

The first time we attended, I was shocked at the intimacy of this moment. We were so close we could match every person's voice to their face. One woman in particular stuck out. She was one of the oldest congregants, a Black woman who stayed seated in her wheelchair while the rest of us stood. As I tried to find my pitch, she got right to singing— loudly and way, way off key. I was caught off guard and distracted by her voice, as it pulled me out of myself and the spiritual moment. Then I looked at her face and the way she was singing so earnestly among the others gathered in that circle, and I realized *this* was the spiritual moment: all of us showing up, imperfect, coming together for second and third and fourth chances, bound to something so much bigger than what any of us were on our own. As I sang with those in that circle, I prayed that my bounds would extend beyond it—to the women of color in my office, to my friends, to the work outside that room.

I would love to end this story by saying that I later told Tiffany how upset her racist comment made me and to never speak like that in my presence again. I regret to say I never did. I left that job and city not long after that interaction. I still think about what I would have said exactly. What I *should* have said. From this exchange I understood more fully what Martin Luther King Jr. likely meant when in his 1967 speech

"Beyond Vietnam—A Time to Break Silence," he said, "In the End, we will remember not the words of our enemies, but the silence of our friends." It wasn't just that I hadn't thought of my Black friends fast enough. There had been something else at play. Something that made me stay silent. Something that Dr. King spoke of before I was even born. What had I been afraid speaking up would do? What exactly did I think it would cost me?

I was learning there was no path I could choose that would be devoid of racism, because *I* was on the path. The work wasn't just out there in the world, fixing broken things. The work was in myself too. And just because I was committed to challenging racism did not automatically mean I would do it at every opportunity. I realized this was going to take a lot more persistence.

4

DO YOU WANT TO GET WELL?

Are you sure, sweetheart, that you want to be well? . . .
Just so's you're sure, sweetheart, and ready to be healed,
cause wholeness is no trifling matter.
A lot of weight when you're well.

TONI CADE BAMBARA

Rarely, if ever, are any of us healed in isolation.
Healing is an act of communion.

BELL HOOKS

JOHN AND I MOVED BACK TO CHICAGO just in time to attend Barack Obama's election night victory in Grant Park. We stood at the edge of the crowd, soaking in the moment. The energy in the air was electric; relief and rejoicing were all rolled up together in the sounds of "Yes we can!" from those around us. I called Katrina the next day, and she told me that she had stood over her baby boy's crib, crying as she told him there was nothing he couldn't do. There was a hope and a sense of change that (it seemed) much of the nation was experiencing. Even so, it felt to me that the church had some catching up to do.

As a newly married couple, John and I started looking for a church to call home. We longed for the diversity of our church in Washington, DC, and apparently, we were not alone in that desire. A study for Lifeway Research found that over 85 percent of Protestant pastors said every church should strive for racial diversity. Yet that same percentage also reported having one predominant racial group in attendance. We considered attending a Black church, although I couldn't shake the comments from a few Black friends who spoke of the safety their Black church provided them, a place out of the White gaze. I had no doubt we would be welcomed, but would that welcoming come at a cost to others?

The church I grew up attending had a reputation for being at the forefront of some relief work through what they called their "compassion and justice" ministry. They had been on the frontlines of the American church's response to the AIDS crisis in Africa and had partnered with a church from one of Chicago's historically Black South Side communities to create their own version of a Sankofa trip. One of the original megachurches in the United States, its White founder had experienced a "second conversion" regarding racism and was committed to pushing his congregation from an "all right with being all White" church to one where diversity was valued. By no means was it a perfect vision, but the promise along with the potential to influence other churches was one of the main reasons I returned—not only as an attender, but on staff where I worked with the team that put on the weekend services.

It was there that Austin and I reunited. We hadn't been in the same city since college, and it felt thrilling, almost providential, that our paths were crossing again. She was hired to provide racial reconciliation training for staff and congregants.

Austin recruited a team of about ten of us from the church staff to create experiential learning events and classes together. There were three Black women, four White women (including myself), one Indian woman, two Black men, and one White man. It was the most diverse team I had ever been a part of, and it provided an environment where we were all pushed to be our most creative selves. This creative push was not unique to our team. According to organizational psychologist Adam Grant,

> When everyone in a group is the same race, they do worse at [creative problem-solving] but they think they do better, because they're more comfortable. Diverse groups are more creative. It's not just because they have access to a wider range of ideas. They feel more uncomfortable, and that discomfort motivates them to do extra preparation and share new information.

We formed some genuine trust by pushing through the discomfort. It didn't hurt that Austin was one of the most collaborative leaders I had ever worked under. She hadn't just assembled this group because of our ethnic diversity; our experiences in human resources, teaching, pastoring, producing, and the arts were all seen as necessities. In other spaces I had been in, differences went unspoken, but here they were seen, celebrated, and utilized.

We met weekly to brainstorm and develop our ideas into something that we could use with the entire staff. Pretty soon, we were regularly sharing articles and definitions and going through some of the exercises ourselves to see which ones were the most helpful, thought-provoking, and challenging. We were the test-takers as well as the test-makers.

It was early 2012, and the country was experiencing the most public reckoning with race that I could remember since I was in elementary school, when Rodney King was caught on tape being beaten severely by four police officers (who were all later acquitted by a nearly all-White jury, setting off the Watts Uprising or the Watts Riots in Los Angeles). The murder of Trayvon Martin, a seventeen-year-old Black boy walking home with a hoodie over his head and Skittles in his pockets, had just occurred and brought to light many assumptions about where we really were in the quest toward equality, equity, and justice.

At one lunch meeting we sat in the basement underneath the sanctuary, all of us comparing notes on what we had brought to eat before moving on to quick highlights from our weekends. That day the conversation turned to one of the first definitions we wanted to teach—racism. Most White Christians we were around did not want to go near this word, instead preferring *prejudice* or *bias*, and we were determined to address that avoidance by including it up front. We shared definitions we had found and crafted a working definition we would share at the next class. One person chimed in with the moving walkway illustration from Beverly Daniel Tatum:

> I sometimes visualize the ongoing cycle of racism as a moving walkway at the airport. Active racist behavior is equivalent to walking fast on the conveyor belt. . . . Passive racist behavior is equivalent to standing still on the walkway. No overt effort is being made, but the conveyor belt moves the bystanders along to the same destination as those who are actively walking. Some of the bystanders may feel the motion of the conveyor belt, see the active racists ahead of them, and choose to turn around. . . . But unless they are walking actively in the opposite direction at a speed faster than the conveyor belt, unless they are actively antiracist, they will find themselves carried along with the others.

It was a profound thought—even if we weren't actively participating in racism, we could still be moving in that direction by not countering it. The person who shared the illustration summed it up for the room by saying, "It's not enough to stand still; we have to turn around and run in the opposite direction."

This comment generated a lot of energized conversation, but when there was a lull, a White woman began to share. "All this time, basically my whole life, and as a Christian, I thought if I just was nice to everyone and treated them all the same, if I was not seeing people's color, that was it. I was not being racist. Problem solved.

"But the more I listen to you all talk, I'm realizing even though I've tried to do that, it hasn't worked. I'm still standing on that moving sidewalk someone mentioned. I'm still racist." She paused as she considered her next few words. "I'm racist." The room stayed mostly quiet, a few of us nodding in understanding as tears ran down her face. The White woman next to her squeezed her hand. The woman didn't appear defeated; in fact her face appeared rather peaceful. No longer fighting the truth but instead taking it by the hand and letting it lead her forward.

Maybe some of the holiest moments exist in church basements. Maybe there is less fear of disappointing God in a church basement—maybe people feel permission to tell the truth. But in that moment, the room turned into a sacred space. Those who are of the Catholic faith or in recovery might be more versed in the power of confession, of saying the quiet parts out loud—the way it releases and frees, the way it calls out the truth and faces reality—so one can shift from hiding to healing. I had felt something similar on Sankofa, a recognition of my own racism that felt less like a sentencing and more like a diagnosis. It was a beginning, not an ending. It was an invitation toward healing, which was, after all, so much of what Jesus was all about.

I have always loved the interaction recorded in John 5 between Jesus and the man lying beside the pool. Unable to walk for thirty-eight years, the man had been coming to this healing water every day for years, hoping for a miracle. As Jesus encountered the man, Jesus could have asked him a lot of questions, or offered sympathy or blessing, or made any number of assumptions. Instead, he asked a question: "Do you want to get well?" (John 5:6 NIV).

Do you want to get well? Our answer should be obvious. But it's not. Getting well is not always an easy or simple process. First, you have to admit to yourself and to those around you that you are not well, or that something is wrong. This is no small thing. Depending on the diagnosis, people may see you differently. There can be shame or stigma around the discovery. Life may look different as you try different medicines, diets, or therapies. But hopefully, you get well. It does not happen overnight. Sometimes, getting well is a short process involving a simple solution. But most often, healing takes time, with much guidance and quite a bit of effort.

Friends of mine recently got some news about their young child receiving an unexpected diagnosis, and they told me that at first they avoided embracing this particular diagnosis because they had heard such hard things about it. But they had come to a breaking point and couldn't keep living as though nothing was different about their child. Accepting the diagnosis meant they had access to more resources and allowed them to find community with other parents facing similar circumstances.

Sitting in the church basement that day, one woman came to her own breaking point during our meeting. The diagnosis of "racist" wasn't the greatest shame anymore. The real shame would have been to keep living as though nothing was different.

The instant this woman said, "I'm racist," the energy of the room shifted for all of us. For some, it was the first time we had heard someone plainly say it, and not surrounded by the words "I'm not racist" (which was almost always followed by something rather racist—sigh). For others, it signified the potential of what we were doing. If we could witness one person move from denial to recognizing racism internally, that helped us envision it playing out across the church. It's one thing to recognize and point your finger at the racism out there in the world, but it's a whole other thing to point it back at yourself. People are usually more comfortable looking outside of themselves as a distraction to avoid looking within. We wanted both. We wanted people to become aware of racism in all its forms, in systems and structures, in hearts and minds, wherever it lived.

● ● ●

Our team provided required trainings for all staff teams and held optional weekly classes for congregants and anyone who was interested. We got people on their feet during our first activity that dealt with stereotypes. Words were written on the church campus conference room walls: *CEO, drug dealer, pastor, prisoner, shoplifter, engineer,* and *doctor.* As the class walked around the room, everyone was prompted to quickly and instinctively press sticky notes with *Black, White,* or *Brown* written on them beside those words. Perhaps the colors were too basic, but we wanted to show the ways we had all been brainwashed when it came to stereotyping and racial profiling. We finished putting up our Post-its and walked around the room to see what everyone's knee-jerk responses resulted in. I was stunned as I walked from word to word—why hadn't the class's diverse ages, races, and life experiences made a difference? Post-it by Post-it revealed the truth: we had been trained into this way of thinking. Caught or taught, it didn't matter. We all responded almost exactly the same way.

Some people in the class were confused that they could even participate in the exercise at all, as they were committed to staying colorblind—they didn't want to see. If some color did creep through, it was the tip of the melanin iceberg—the easy, the entertaining, the feel good, the celebratory. In fact, during one class, a White woman raised her hand and shared with the group how much this was impossible for her, how she had prided herself on treating everyone equally no matter the color of their skin, how she "could only see people according to the color of their personality."

"So if I asked you to close your eyes and tell me the color of my skin, you wouldn't be able to do that?" Austin asked.

"No," she responded quickly. "Because I don't know you on the inside yet. When I learn your personality then I will be able to see you how I see other people—as red and purple and blue and green. In fact, once I was on the train and a new friend of mine kept calling my name, but I couldn't tell it was her because her color blended in with everyone else that was a stranger to me. I felt bad later when I realized I had been ignoring her."

If you think this sounds a little odd, you are not alone. This woman sounded proud of this puzzling story and proud of appearing colorblind. Perhaps because she was twisting the golden rule from how others wanted to be treated into how she wanted to be treated. And seen. As a unique individual. I almost wanted Austin to repeat her question just to make sure everyone else in the room could see that standing in front of them was a Black woman. That they wouldn't need to write it on their hand to remember or sneak one more look to double check. And that there was nothing wrong with seeing her color. What was wrong was treating her unfairly because of her color. Which is partially why the idea of being colorblind has risen in popularity since the concept was introduced in the 1970s; we have been offered the perspective that being colorblind means everyone is treated the same. By each other and by our institutions. Spoiler—it does not in fact pan out that way.

Can we just pause and reflect on how strange it is that the idea of being colorblind is not only tolerated but also has been embraced and championed for so long? Every time I think it's over, I hear another (likely White) person speaking of its virtue. To believe that being aware of race or racism means you are racist—and then to claim to be color-blind, convinced that you are doing the right thing—is prevalent and problematic.

● ● ●

I couldn't stop thinking about that woman's comment. *I felt bad later when I realized I had been ignoring her.* It unlocked something important for my own understanding. At the end of the day, colorblindness is not occurring; color-ignoring is, and it's often ignorable only by White people who experience (often invisible to us) privileges related to being White. In his book *How To Be An Antiracist*, Dr. Ibram Kendi explores what occurs when we attempt to solve racism by ignoring race, or acting colorblind: "Assimilationists believe in the post-racial myth that talking about race constitutes racism, or that if we stop identifying by race, then racism will miraculously go away." I can understand this logic, this way of thinking that if you eliminate the problem then you've got the solution. But the problem has never been race. The problem has always been racism. Racism came first. As author Ta-Nehisi Coates so bluntly put it, "race is the child of racism, not the father."

Race was created to do the work of racism, dehumanization, exploitation, power abuse, rape, and stripping people of their histories and rights and humanity—not the other way around. Let's not ever forget that. Racism came first, and the sorting of people into racial categories with differing values was created to accomplish its dirty work.

It can be confusing because race itself is not objectively real, not in the way we often talk about it; it's not biological but instead a social construct that breaks down easily when you start to poke at it. Let me explain it this way: I once heard a story about a young child who asked her mom why someone we call Black might have lighter skin than someone of Italian descent that we consider White. "Aren't we all just different shades of Brown?" she asked. This kid was on to the inconsistency of the labels of race, because we aren't consistently using racial terms to discuss someone's literal appearance. Whereas racism is very much objectively real, being the basis of institutions, laws, and aspects of our lives big and small.

Kendi continues that when we attempt to be colorblind, what ends up happening isn't the end of racism, because

> if we stop using racial categories, then we will not be able to identify racial inequity. If we cannot identify racial inequity, then we will not be able to identify racist policies. If we cannot identify racist policies, then we cannot challenge racist policies. If we cannot challenge racist policies, then racist power's final solution will be achieved: a world of inequity none of us can see, let alone resist.

If we can't see something we can't say something, and the cycles of racism continue unchallenged and unchanged. I wondered if we White people really just wanted to avoid seeing what our White identity did for us. And how for many people of color, their racial identity was more knowingly connected to their overall identity than we even realized? That some of us could more easily color-ignore?

The next class, we asked everyone to write out the ten most important parts of their identity. We gave a few examples to help get the ball rolling. I was not facilitating this part of the class, so I sat with the other attendees and wrote things like my name, my gender, my faith affiliation, my roles in my family and at work, and nearly last on the list, my race. Other people put similar things as well as athletics they participated in, the region they grew up in, a skill they possessed, or a hobby they loved.

We were instructed to cross off the things on our list one by one until we were left with the top two. It honestly was incredibly challenging to answer the question "Who am I really?" We were then invited to share what was left and why. I struggled with choosing between my being a woman and my faith. They both felt like the most accurate anchors of my identity reflected in a single word. If it hadn't been a race class that I helped lead, I honestly don't know if I would have listed White at all. It wasn't there at the halfway point when I got down to my top five. Other White people shared similar results as we went around the room.

But that wasn't the case for the people of color in the group—almost everyone shared their final two were between their faith and their racial identity, and that they really wouldn't know how to eliminate either group. Even though they loved and practiced their faith every day, their memories and stories were more colored *by* their color.

Other than the woman who claimed she couldn't see color, the rest of us were getting well practiced at seeing and naming the connection between color, identity, and stereotypes and the ways we noticed and ignored it. Now, people were asking the age-old question that is inevitable when folks get all fired up: "But what do we do?"

"You keep going," Austin told them.

So they did. I did too. I wanted to keep getting well.

5

LOSING MY MARBLES

Not everything that is faced can be changed, but nothing can be changed until it is faced.

JAMES BALDWIN

THE NEXT WEEK OUR TEAM SET UP THE ROOM with round tables. At each table was a bowl filled with hundreds of glass marbles and a small, empty plastic container in front of each chair. Our team had come to rely on shared experiences as a jumping off point for introspection and discussion, and tonight's class was no different. As our last class ended with people insisting we tell them what to do next, we figured it wise to literally show them what they already had been doing—daily choices that kept them standing still on the moving walkway. My teammate Ashlee explained to the group what we were about to do.

"In front of you are two piles of marbles, each pile a different color. We are going to ask a series of questions that all pertain to your normal daily life. The marbles will represent your answers," she began. I looked down at the bowl of marbles and selected blue to represent my White race and yellow for answers that represented all other races. I assured those at my table that it would make sense once we started.

"Here is the first question: 'The last three families you hosted in your home were . . .' So now you put in one marble for each family or person depending solely on their race—make sense? Don't overthink it. Be honest. Let's get started!" We then gave the group the following list:

- The last three families you hosted in your home were . . .
- The three most-played movies in your home are . . .
- The three most-watched television shows in your home are . . .
- The last three books you read are written by . . .
- Your three closest neighbors are . . .
- The elementary, middle, and high schools you attended were . . .

Plunk, plunk, plunk went the marbles into the clear jars.

The first racial reconciliation exercise I ever experienced happened before Sankofa, during my freshman year in college. It was basically a "welcome to college in Chicago" course they made everyone take. They lined us all up in our university classroom and asked questions like, "Did you have more than fifty books in your home growing up?" and "Did you learn about the history of people that looked like you in a positive way in your elementary school history classes?" If the answer was yes, we were invited to take a step forward. Then there were statements like, "If you have never had a teacher of your same race, take a step backward." I would learn later that we had just done a "privilege walk." I had no choice in my answers; my stepping forward and backward as I used my body to respond to the questions was the only way I had participated. Every answer had been handed to me, for better and, for many others in the classroom, for worse. I experienced a very quick range of emotions: at first, my competitive nature was excited that I was able to step forward—it felt like winning, one of my very favorite things. That feeling of victory quickly moved to guilt as I looked around and saw the clear line between the White students and students of color.

Intended or not, the impact of that exercise was a feeling of powerlessness. No matter what we did in that moment, we couldn't change our answer for "Yes, my grandparents went to college," or "Nope, I've never been told that I am a credit to my race," or "Yep, we can call 911 without fear of the police arriving at our home." While we were taking steps forward and backward, we were all actually stuck, our bodies bound by the roots of systems and structures that were in motion no matter what.

As I looked around the room at the jars filled with mostly one color (representing anything but a colorblind choice), it really struck me. So often White people's initial resistance against seeing racism clearly was an insistence that they "hadn't done anything." I had certainly wrestled with that knee-jerk response. And if you looked only at an activity like the privilege walk, you could kind of see their point—because that is exactly the point. But I appreciate how Tori Douglass from White Homework explains privilege: "You don't need to be the thief to materially benefit from the theft." We don't do anything to receive whatever innate privileges we possess. They are unearned advantages that oftentimes no one is asking us to notice, let alone examine.

I realize *privilege* can be a tricky word, that it might elicit an image of (depending on one's age) *Lifestyles of the Rich and Famous* or *MTV Cribs* or *Million Dollar Listing* or billionaires traveling to outer space. It doesn't have to be that extreme or only about money. And it doesn't mean life is never hard; it's just never harder, entirely because of the specific privileges we were given. By design, privilege often feels invisible in the ways that we have it.

Eleanor Roosevelt is famous for many things, but in my house it's mostly for her often repeated quote, "Comparison is the thief of joy." Maybe the slight modification is that when it comes to understanding privilege, comparison is actually an invitation to respond with enjoyment or examination.

I've seen both responses.

Once I co-led a privilege walk for a group of high school students. When it was over, I invited the students to share in one word how they initially felt after looking around the room and seeing where they and others ended up. Most emotions they listed involved feeling sad, mad, or confused, until one White teenage boy expressed a different feeling. "Blessed," he told the group, standing from the very front of the line.

I tried to keep my face from falling as his light hazel eyes lingered on mine. My mind raced. He hadn't just thrown out a word like *lucky*—for many, a synonym for blessing. He had said "blessed" as part of a framework many Christians appear to operate within: everything we have been given comes from God and is therefore ours to enjoy. Verses in Genesis, telling us we have "dominion" or rule over the earth, and James 1:17, declaring "every perfect gift is from above, coming down from the Father," are sometimes used to defend privilege as something intended by the God of the universe. How could one argue with that? And if you were the "blessed one," why would you want to argue with that?

If you were a prominent White pastor from Atlanta, you wouldn't. One such pastor made headlines when, in a conversation on racism, he argued that White people "miss the blessing of slavery, that it actually built up the framework for the world that White people live in." He also pushed against the use of the word *privilege* and wanted to replace it with "White blessing." This idea is not solely his, nor is it new; the concept of "blessing" has been used to defend all sorts of things, including the slave trade out of Africa many generations ago.

Another privilege walk ended with one White man feeling so guilty, he shut down for the rest of the conversation. He had gone his whole life thinking his status and position was his and his alone, tied only to a strong work ethic and some serious talent. He was overwhelmed by the idea that his winning was actually directly and traceably tied to holding others back, to something that kept others losing.

I wouldn't lead or recommend a privilege walk anymore. While I think it is an incredibly effective way to see what is often unseen, anything the White participants learn does not justify or excuse the cost to the people of color in the room. But it was the closest I've ever been to witnessing people understand being White. And not just "Oh, I have less melanin in my peach skin," but, "Look at how everyone who is White answered these questions. I am part of something bigger than me, something called *Whiteness*." But what even is "Whiteness"?

This is where you get to choose your own adventure (Remember those books? I loved them so much). If you would like the more academic definition of Whiteness, please keep reading the rest of this paragraph. If you would like my much simpler definition, skip to the next paragraph. Here goes: The invention of race as a means to divide and group people in a societal hierarchy began to be developed in the 1500s. Tied to the creation of race as a means to access one's humanity, the concept of Whiteness was devised to create a deliberate hierarchy between the workers taken from Europe and Africa in order to define who was fully human, and therefore privileged, and who was property. For the first time, even the poorest White person now had an immediate advantage over someone considered Black. Activist Paul Kivel put it this way: "Whiteness is a constantly shifting boundary separating those who are entitled to have certain privileges from those whose exploitation and vulnerability to violence is justified by their not being White."

And here's my much simpler definition: Whiteness is when being White is the default, the normal, the catered to, the prioritized, the best.

For many White people, it took us slowing down and answering questions during a walk to recognize our Whiteness. I witnessed some White people make sense of their newly realized White status by seeing their privileges as a blessing they dare not challenge. For others, their renegotiations and understanding led them to feel deeply responsible, racked with guilt and shame, and like they were unable to do anything right. I fell into the latter. There is great power in shame, but learning rooted in shame does not foster growth and evolution.

According to shame and vulnerability researcher, professor, and author Dr. Brené Brown, "Shame is a tool of oppression—it will never be an effective social justice tool, ever. It is the tool of stigmatizing, reducing, dehumanizing. . . . Shame is the tool of the patriarchy, it's the tool of nationalism, it's the tool of supremacy. Why would we ever pick it up to dismantle those things?" The more I learn about shame and justice, the more I understand that they do not belong together. I'm happy to report I'm not alone.

I think there is this belief that if we just get White people feeling bad and guilty enough and riddled with shame, we will finally start the work of addressing racism. But it doesn't work like that. At least not for a long enough amount of time to really make a difference. It doesn't work in any other area of our lives. Why would we think this would bring the masses to justice instead of doubling down and running in the opposite direction, instead of leading us to become numb and ignore the pain and realities altogether? It's akin to a fad diet motivated by an unhealthy desire for overnight results—likely rooted more in self-loathing than love and care for the body. When I am taking the best care of my body, it is rooted in deep love and appreciation. Love and purpose keep me going, not contempt.

I'm not suggesting we let facing one's privilege and supremacy be easy. However, when we leave people with only the concept of "I am racist *but* with no possibility of change—period," they are cut off from movement, transformation, and growth. We are relying on the tool of shame. When we instead expose the truth and move to the reality of "I am racist *and* there are things I can do to challenge that," it gives us somewhere to go. There can and should be deep feelings of sadness, discomfort, grief, and yes, guilt, but the end goal is movement away from those racist thoughts and repeated and unchecked actions, not the sinking feeling that there is no way out. Anything that encourages static behavior—that is not constantly pushing and pulling and sometimes dragging us toward something better—is not the target.

A few years ago, I took a writing class at improv holy grail The Second City in Chicago, where so many of our comedic heroes began. I learned about different setups in comedy and the improv classic "yes, and." In any improv interaction, the goal is to keep the story moving forward, so when your partner says, "This disco-tech is lame," you don't say, "We're not in a disco-tech, we're at my mom's retirement party!" Instead, you say, "Totally. Hey, wait a second, is that your boss dancing on the bar?" Otherwise the sketch is dead; because instead of "yes, and"-ing, you "no, but"-ed. Momentum over. Laughs gone.

No one wants a "no, but" partner. Not in improv games and not in the work around race and privilege. Accepting reality and then adding to it is the only way to move things forward.

"I'm a privileged White woman, *but* I've worked really hard for everything I've got" versus "*Yes*, I am a privileged White woman, *and* here are the ways I work to share my current privileges and advocate for a whole new system altogether."

What a difference. When in doubt, remember *ands* are better than *buts*.

● ● ●

At the end of the marble exercise, we sat around the tables and looked at our jars—evidence of the sobering reality that the worlds we had created, the ones we had a lot of say in, mostly looked only like ourselves. Up until now, many hadn't really noticed. Or felt like anything was missing. Or realized how many choices we had made that were racialized. It's like when you get to the checkout line at Target and the total comes to over one hundred dollars, and you're thinking, "I just came in for shampoo and toothpaste." Our choices added up, and we were getting hit with the total cost. It didn't really matter that anyone "felt" like they lived a diverse life. The proof was in the marbles.

We sat in silence for a minute, realizing that one book by the Black author we read or that one African American museum we went to for Martin Luther King Jr. Day hadn't changed up the results. The bowl we were looking at wasn't a melting pot; those marbles weren't going to spill over and influence the others inside. This wasn't dominoes with one toppling down the next, resulting in unstoppable movement. And yet there was a story held within these marbles, a story that we could either challenge or continue. After all, if nothing changes, nothing changes.

There was some defensiveness at first and even some pushback on the questions—"What's a White magazine, anyway?" someone asked.

Our team took turns adding to our answer: "Well, who is it for? If you say 'everyone,' keep digging. Who is on the cover? Who is the editor-in-chief? What are the topics and values it upholds? If you are feeling defensive, let's remember this is not an attack on White people; it's an interrogation of Whiteness, of what's become the standard, of who is centered and who is pushed to the margins or kept off the page altogether."

It would be naive and potentially even dangerous to think that the work of justice and liberation for all people will happen because our marble jars are diverse. We weren't training White people to get better at buying issues of *Essence* instead of *Vogue*. We weren't trying to have people meet some quota or percentage. No one was looking at my jar impressed that I had invited a friend of color over for dinner last week or that my nightstand book pile was full of women of color authors. This was bigger than that. This was a chance to look at how seemingly small, innocent choices were maintained. If we stayed so colorblind we couldn't see that Whiteness had infiltrated our magazines, would we ever see how it moved in more important spaces like our education and justice systems, the health care industry and our churches? Would we choose differently when the stakes were much higher than where to order takeout?

Transforming the world takes time, and it most likely starts with making choices to transform our own lives. While the privilege walk showed how little is up to us, there is so much that is on our watch, ready to be repeated or disrupted. Where can we use our power to be part of fixing what is broken?

We get to decide. We have a choice.

We can hoard our privileges and keep our marbles, or we can decide to reject the standards of Whiteness and work to multiply our advantages, turning them into rights enjoyed by all people. It can be scary to feel like we are losing our marbles, to feel like we are leaving behind where we have always fit in or been understood or excelled. I'm begging you to let that go. Because the marbles you gain will propel you forward.

Instead of comfort you will step into wonder. You will lose approval with some people as you no longer fit in with them, and gain belonging with those who see the person you are becoming. You will trade your fear of change for an embrace of growth, and experience the shedding of stagnant and selfish ideas to make space for the more beautiful, the more generous, the more transformative ones. You have the power to let go. You will lose marbles but I'm willing to bet any you lose will be replaced with something so much better. It's up to you. What's it gonna be?

6

INSERT TOKEN TO PLAY

Where there is no vision, the people perish.

PROVERBS 29:18 (KJV)

FOR A LONG TIME, "WHY?" has been my favorite question. Maybe it's the theater kid in me. I want to get to the heart of it all, to the thing beneath the thing. "Why am I doing this?" or "What's my motivation?" always helped me understand the character I played and the world I inhabited (fictional and real). Finding my why was often at the center of any important choice or decision in my life. It gave me a stronger and more thoroughly examined foundation to stand on.

Which was why it was so unlike me when I didn't stop and consider why people should want the contents of their marble jar to change in the first place. I assumed it was because they were trying to challenge Whiteness, trying to remember that White didn't have to be the default. It didn't dawn on me that some were motivated by a reason they couldn't exactly pin down themselves. Or worse, they were motivated primarily by optics.

My role at the church (besides handing out marbles to folks) was as a creative producer. Basically anything creative that happened at a church service, I helped bring to life. The church had a long history of using the arts to engage those in attendance in unique ways. It was one of the things I had loved about it so much growing up—I could show up to church and hear a Dave Matthews Band cover (don't judge) or watch the story of the prodigal son depicted through a drama.

The very first service I attended when I was interviewing for my job was during Martin Luther King Jr. weekend, and I was inspired and challenged by its message and creativity. So after I was hired and in the room where it happened, I began to notice something: the majority of the team planning the MLK services was White. That's because the majority of the team planning every service was White, because the majority of the staff was, you guessed it, White. The elders were all White; everyone on executive leadership was White. The only place that wasn't majority White was the congregation and the worship team.

For years, those MLK weekends stood apart; the entirety of the church's reconciliation and diversity values weighed heavily on that service's wee little shoulders. For one weekend a year, the voices and opinions and ideas of our (few) Black staff were invited in, listened to, submitted to, and held with higher respect. Then, like clockwork, services resumed the usual pattern. And that started feeling stranger and stranger to me. Why didn't we invite them to the table the next week when it was back to a regular weekend? Why did it always go back to the way it had always been? Why did White people own who was invited in the first place? And why was a table filled with White people planning fifty-one services a year just considered something to be *aware* of instead of a problem to solve? When awareness doesn't lead to action, what's the point?

As I sat with those questions, something became painfully clear: for some of the White people around me, appearance was often the motive for change. We usually stopped short of fixing an occurrence of racism and instead focused on just an appearance of it. It wasn't uncommon (or unencouraged) to hear things like:

"What will it look like to have an all-White worship team? Let's make sure we have some diversity on the stage."

"The whole conference lineup can't be White men. How will that look? We need at least one woman or person of color."

"It's Hispanic Heritage Month, so we need at least one song in Spanish for every service."

At one meeting, three of my coworkers and I sat around a table. Halfway through the meeting, our music director, the only Black person in the room, pushed his cellphone to the center of the worn wood table we were all gathered around. "8 Ways People of Color Are Tokenized in Nonprofits" was bolded at the top of the page. The author was Helen Kim Ho, an attorney, activist, and diversity life coach who was calling out workplaces supposedly doing the most good.

I took the phone and started scrolling. "I have felt every single one of these here," our music director said as I read. I nodded in agreement as each point brought up a thought or memory of something I had witnessed but had never been the direct recipient of.

1. You recruit POC [People of Color] to formal leadership positions, but keep all the power.

2. Your paid staff in charge of messaging are White, and your volunteer storytellers are POC.

3. You only hire People of Color for "POC" stuff.

I stopped scrolling. This was exactly why this process had always felt off, I realized.

One key thing I've learned from others in the work of justice is to consider intent versus impact. Where intent and motivation are explored through asking *why*, asking *what* gets to the impact. It goes a step beyond simply getting curious about something and helps provide a clearer understanding of what is actually occurring, because there are most likely layers to these events. We must unpack them in order to see better.

If involving more Black staff than normal in the creative process was (and I'm using air quotes quite deliberately here) "with good intentions," but the impact was people feeling tokenized, disempowered, and being asked to speak for more than just themselves (because people of color are not a monolith, all thinking and believing the same things), then what's the significance of the intent? Not only do the ends not justify the means, the means might actually be mean. Could it be true that we White people around the circle wanted not just the addition of ideas but a sign-off on the whole thing? That, if need be, we could reference them by saying, "It wasn't just us who liked this idea—Sharon and Alisha and Tracy signed off on it too."

A lot of misunderstandings I've witnessed often come down to White people being so focused on their intentions that it allows little room to unpack the impact for the people of color. When someone steps on your foot in a crowded room, it doesn't hurt any less just because you understand it wasn't done on purpose. And when the person whose foot is bleeding from being stomped on is less cared for than the stomper, that is textbook supremacy; the cries of regret or "unintention" overshadows the actual pain and problem.

There were other White people who I believed were earnestly trying to grow away from idolizing Whiteness. Some had participated in the marble jar activity, and when they saw the physical representation of their choices, they had a real desire to change their future decisions. This is where there can be a rub: they know something is not right about having an all-White marble jar, but they're not sure why. Instead of getting reflective about why their choices often skew White, many people get reactive and simply try to change the contents of the jar. When the choices are around what books and movies are in their home, the opportunity for harm is very low. When the choices involve inviting people into their lives and hiring at their companies, the chance for harm to them (likely unintended) increases. When there is no vision for this changed behavior, people can experience real harm.

Could it be that we White people want the appearance of diversity but never at any cost, especially the cost of control or power? Could it be that we believe no one is missing around the table, that those representing the best ideas are there and if we extend an invitation outside of that, it's because we are doing them a favor out of generosity? Those are bold statements, but I have seen their validity up close. I have at times felt them. We love the idea of diversity when we control what it means. We

love to cast diversity but usually stop there, not wanting to be changed
or challenged by it.

I know this too well. For a long time, I was complicit in perpetuating tokenism. There is a fuzzy line between that and representation.
Throughout my career as a video producer, I got used to hearing the
directive from my various bosses to make sure the video was "diverse"
and "inclusive." When talking through a project, part of the conversation was making sure the video never had an all-White cast. As
I learned more about my responsibility in avoiding tokenism, I
tried something different. I was casting a video for a non-MLK, non-
heritage celebration month service. I had a list from the casting
agency with each person's picture, and I was determined to go beyond
the one or two token Black people to make sure a White cast didn't
dominate. One by one, the people came for their time slot. The first
few were White, and then the next six or seven were Black and Asian
and Latinx.

At the end of the day, we had filmed with a half-White, half people of
color cast—which was perhaps expected on MLK weekend when we
were highlighting the value of diversity, but to just highlight it through
action with no explanation wasn't really our style. "I never thought I
would say we needed more White people for a project," someone joked
on set. There seemed to be a tipping point where it became "too diverse"
for some folks.

How did I finally conclude that this was tokenism? Because we
weren't asking this question of diversity and inclusion in any other
spaces. I would not have done my job well if I cast all White people,
and yet our human resources team was not held to this standard for
hires, nor was there any disruption to a process where, year after year,
only new White people were elected to the elder board. These questions were only asked for the easiest and most visible choices our
institution made.

Tokenism is sneaky. Writer Helen Kim Ho defines tokenism as
"covert racism":

Racism requires those in power to maintain their privilege by exercising social, economic and/or political muscle against people of color (POC). Tokenism achieves the same while giving those in power the appearance of being non-racist and even champions of diversity because they recruit and use POC as racialized props.

When someone is turned into a prop, they are turned from a person into a thing, and in this case, a sort of symbol or mascot. There was something especially tragic about this occurring at a church, where people were refusing the concept of the *imago Dei*, all of us made in the image of God. Much of my life I had heard of Black people "playing the race card"—the idea that a person attempts to unfairly win an argument by bringing up race in a space where it poses no relevance to the situation. Sheree Atcheson directly addresses this in her brilliant article for *Forbes*: "To discount race in how we all live, work and exist would be facetious. This is why the statement 'playing the race card' is simply a derailment tactic."

We don't play racism with cards; we often play it with tokens.

Let me be very clear that the people it hurts the most are the ones being tokenized. And, unfortunately, they are not the only ones impacted. I think many of us have been played by this type of racism for a really long time. I was for much of my life. Having a person of color to point to and show off a value. Played. Feeling less able to critique an organization because they have a diversity council. Played. Thinking that someone is moving their business toward antiracist practices because of certain phrases in their mission statement or models in their marketing campaigns. Played.

I now realize I wasn't just played, though. I was trained.

Seeing three White men in a row lead parts of the meeting followed by one White woman. Or two White men speaking at church while an Asian or Black man leads the congregation in worship: "See, it's not all White. We're doing all right." Trained. A sense of relief when the third person in the commercial or video is Black, Indigenous, Asian, or Latinx.

Trained. When the cast of a show has one friend or adopted child of color. Trained.

Just enough color to let out any pangs of pressure.

I'm learning to be suspicious of anything that takes the pressure off of the urgency for justice. Anything that signals to my brain that "It's not that bad" and "See, it's getting better. You don't have to raise your concern at the next meeting or send that email or sign that petition. Progress is happening. It starts with one person—which is better than nothing!"

The pursuit of justice is hard and, I would argue, may need to occur without the optics of diversity. The pursuit of diversity is easier, and, when not chasing justice, is filled with people of color being tokenized, intended and not. True diversity makes movements stronger, while token diversity cheapens and detracts from momentum and ends up hurting a lot more than helping. If we want to get to a better vision, we've got to start asking better questions.

7

EVERYWHERE IS A CRIME SCENE

Later, when I hear others dismissing our voices, our protests for equity by saying "all lives matter" or "blue lives matter," I will wonder how many White Americans are dragged out of their beds in the middle of the night because they might fit a vague description offered up by god knows who. How many skinny, short, blonde men were rounded up when Dylann Roof massacred people in prayer?

PATRISSE CULLORS-BRIGNAC

"HERE WE ARE. CHARLESTON, SOUTH CAROLINA. Or, as I like to call it, home sweet home," our colleague said as our planning team of six arrived at the airport. We were in Charleston to test some locations for a future Sankofa-type trip for our church staff and congregation. Walking out of the terminal, we looked like a United Colors of Benetton ad—a Black woman, an Asian woman, a Latina woman, an Asian man, a Black man, and a White woman, me. Our tour guide was also part of our church staff—coming to Charleston was largely his idea since he knew the area well and had many connections we could leverage. It also had become a focal point in the ongoing national conversation on racism, as just a few months before we arrived, nine Black members of a beloved local church had been targeted and killed while attending a Bible study.

This was my first opportunity to help plan a trip like the one I had been on in college. I knew it was important to expose people to experiences that would provide plenty of aha moments and wear down their well-worn beliefs. As soon as we left the airport in our ten-passenger van, pressure started to build.

It began when we arrived at the Historic Westside neighborhood and walked down Ashley Avenue toward the Charleston Hanging Tree, which was so large that the street was literally paved around it. This was where Denmark Vesey and thirty-four of his followers were lynched. Vesey was an African American leader who worked as a carpenter in Charleston. In June 1822 he was accused and convicted of leading "the rising," a potentially major slave revolt that was scheduled to take place in the city that July.

A teammate suggested we take a picture, but as someone pulled out their camera, all I could imagine was the aftermath of this mass lynching nearly two hundred years ago: a crowd of White people smiling in front of thirty-five dangling Black bodies. I started walking down the road, not sure where I was going, just needing to create physical distance between myself and that image. But the invisible thread connecting the past and the present—between me, Denmark Vesey, his followers, and his executors—was still there.

We arrived at our next destination an hour later. I looked out the van window at the dusty, grassy, unassuming side street behind a run-down pawn shop—the site where a fifty-year-old man named Walter Scott had been shot and killed during an encounter with police over his alleged broken taillight. I pulled up the video of his killing on my phone just to get my bearings. An image of this exact location came up—with a White officer prepared to fire his weapon at the Black man running from him about fifteen feet away. I couldn't bring myself to press play.

A few from our group got out of the van while my friend Ashlee and I stayed in the back.

"Do you think they see that man?" Ashlee whispered. I looked where she was pointing and saw a White man from the pawn shop walk outside.

"I don't think so," I said. "And I just noticed all those 'no trespassing' signs. I have the sense that we're not the first people to park here since Walter Scott was killed."

We watched while a minute passed, maybe more. Our eyes darted back and forth between our team and the man who was watching them. My heart started to beat faster, and I was suddenly cold with fear. I associated this space with trauma and tragedy, and I was afraid that, at any moment, history could repeat itself.

Our group outside noticed the man and started walking back to the van, except for one woman who was lagging behind taking pictures.

As our group members hopped inside the van, I cracked open the window. "Hey, it's time to go!" I yelled, hoping my voice was loud enough for her to hear without reaching the man. I wasn't the only one who felt our presence was a risk, as others in my car joined me in yelling for her return. I willed her to turn around.

The van started to move slowly in her direction. She finally noticed she was by herself outside and casually made her way back to us. I looked away from her and made eye contact with the man before he turned and walked back into his shop. I exhaled, relieved that we were all safe. And I realized maybe I hadn't been yelling after my friend. Maybe I had been yelling after Walter Scott, trying to warn him that he was in danger. But it was too late.

As we drove to our next destination, my mind wandered back to one of the planning meetings we'd had before we arrived in Charleston.

Several people on our team had recently returned from a trip to Israel/Palestine where the goal was to develop a "pro-Israel/pro-Palestine/pro-peace" outlook, rooted in the reality that the conflict in the Middle East is incredibly layered and complex with excruciating pain on both sides. Our team members spent time with people who had lost children at the hands of Israeli soldiers and Palestinian citizens. Even though the reality of the situation is one marked by an imbalance of power, they were inspired by resisting simple "bad/good/right/wrong" thinking as they learned the history and witnessed present-day outcomes in the region. They returned from the trip with a better understanding of both sides' viewpoints.

At our planning meeting, the only White man in the room suggested we take this approach on our Charleston trip by meeting with a Black civil rights advocate and an openly White supremacist—to "hear from" and "understand" both sides.

Perhaps he saw this as a good idea since both sides felt abstract and distant from his own experience. But one thing I've learned is that when we see White supremacy as "out there" instead of within, we will almost always compare ourselves to someone more extreme.

During this meeting I was sitting next to Ashlee, a Black woman who knew intimately the source for this idea since she had also been on an Israel/Palestine trip a year earlier. As soon as the idea was suggested, it seemed to hover over the table. There were murmurs of interest—clearly a very "provocative" idea, some said. Ashlee looked up from her notebook, pen still in hand, motionless. "I won't be attending a meeting like that," she said, although her expression conveyed: *My humanity is not up for debate, and I refuse to be offered as a sacrifice in an attempt to change one person's mind.*

It reminded me of a quote from Dr. King that I first saw on a bumper sticker on my college campus: "Peace is not simply the absence of conflict, but the existence of justice for all people." Dr. King came from a long line of preachers, and his commitment to civil rights was rooted in his faith. I sometimes wonder how many times he read the biblical prophets, who said things like, "They have treated my people's brokenness superficially, claiming, 'Peace, peace,' when there is no peace" (Jeremiah 6:14 CSB).

Peace cannot coexist with injustice. Peace will not come from superficial expressions or at the expense of trauma and pain for the most marginalized. No justice, no peace.

● ● ●

Our team squeezed around two small tables in the middle of a crowded restaurant, surrounded by the smell of fried chicken and sweet tea. We were joined by two Black police officers our host knew in an attempt to "hear from both sides"—but in this case, our guests represented both sides as Black men and police officers. They worked for the same police precinct in Charleston.

The conversation started with the shooting of Walter Scott from earlier this year. Neither of our guests had known the officer who killed Scott.

"What did you think when you heard about it?" our host asked.

"It's complicated," said one of our guests. "Am I surprised that a White police officer shot and killed an unarmed Black man and then tried to cover it up? In some ways, no. A lot of these cops are undoubtedly racist. I've definitely experienced microaggressions and worse from other officers."

Someone else at our table asked if they could talk about the mass shooting and hate crime committed by self-described White supremacist Dylann Roof at the majority-Black church Mother Emanuel, which had occurred just four months ago in June.

Colleagues of theirs, called to the scene in the aftermath, shared that what they saw that night was "horrific." Our guests explained, "For almost fourteen hours, we didn't know where the killer was. Those were some of the most terrifying hours of our lives." They hadn't known if this was part of a larger attack on other Black churches and parts of Charleston or if this was an isolated event. Searching for the killer had felt like trying to find a needle in a haystack. They finally found him about two hundred miles away from the church.

"I heard he confessed he almost didn't go through with it because everyone was so nice to him—but he decided he had to go through with what he called his mission," our guests said.

When police found Dylann Roof, he, like Walter Scott, was pulled over at a traffic stop. They found a gun in his car. Unlike Walter Scott, Roof was brought safely to jail and even stopped for a burger on the way.

We finished our meal and thanked the officers for their time. Then we headed to Emanuel AME Church to attend the same Wednesday night

Bible study that had ended in tragedy just a few months earlier. I noticed a single police car parked at the lot next door. We entered the church through the side of the building. I would later see pictures of Roof entering through this same door.

Ashlee and I made our way down the stairs into the church basement. On the way to the bathroom, I noticed a young, White female police officer.

"I am feeling so nervous," I said as I tried to shake the nerves from my body. "It just feels so surreal to be here. And I can't tell if seeing that police officer makes me feel better or worse. Like, why is she here?"

"It's hard not to keep thinking 'if these walls could talk,'" Ashlee said. "I can feel my imagination running absolutely wild. So I'm just going to try to take a deep breath and be as present as possible tonight."

The Bible study at Emanuel AME Church occurred every Wednesday night from 8-9 p.m. On that night in June when nine church members, including the pastor, were killed, there were just twelve people, all Black, in attendance—thirteen if you counted Roof. Tonight, the two aisles of fifteen rows each were full; the brown folding chairs held White bodies and Black bodies and Brown bodies. I was immediately suspicious of every White person in the room.

We sat three rows from the front. I would learn later that Roof sat in the row ahead of ours. There weren't enough chairs for everyone as more and more people filled the room.

As the service started, so did my need to see the whole room. I began a steady rotation—I looked at the pastor, glanced at the clock, checked in on the officer, and scanned the back door. Look. Glance. Check. Scan. Again and again I did this. Each time, I willed the clock to move faster. The study started with some singing. I couldn't tell you what songs they were. I knew them, and it's a miracle I was able to sing along. I was anything but present.

We moved to an opening prayer and the reading of a few Scriptures. The pastor was new to his position, hired in direct response to the events of the shooting. His newness didn't show. He was pastoral and engaged in the work of the evening. Directly behind him was a large photograph of the nine people who were murdered, many of them older Black women in their sixties and seventies. In one report, Roof said he did it because "y'all raping our women and taking over the world."

Roof didn't come to this conclusion of his own accord. These innocent people are so clearly a stand-in for a long-held fictitious crusade to protect "our" (as Roof implied) White women, to punish Black men and the Black women who raise and love them, and to stop fears of being replaced.

I noticed a few White men come in. They spoke to the police officer, and she left the room. I strained to hear where she had gone, unsure if her presence or absence was better. Had these men lured her into a trap? My heart pounded and my hands started to sweat as I convinced myself this was part of some plan. I was braced for another shooting.

As I continued looking around the room, I noticed for the first time the White man who sat directly behind me. He barely looked up from writing in his notebook. He wrote during the rather lengthy prayer; I knew because of course I wasn't praying with my eyes shut (but believe me, I was praying). He wrote as others sang and when the police officer returned without incident. My scan now went from the pastor to the clock to the White man. Pastor. Clock. White man. In my paranoid state, I imagined he was writing some sort of last-minute manifesto. I willed myself to stay still instead of getting up and walking outside.

Then finally, the pastor said, "The Lord bless you and keep you." My scan rotation began to slow.

"The Lord make his face shine upon you." Pastor.

"And be gracious to you." Clock.

"The Lord lift up his countenance upon you." White man.

"And give you peace." Pastor.

"Amen," I heard myself and others reply.

I exhaled after practically holding my breath for the past hour. People got to their feet and introduced themselves to each other. I couldn't find the strength to stand quite yet. Ashlee stayed seated next to me. "How was that for you?" I asked in a slight whisper, not wanting to be overheard. "Are you as relieved as I am that it's over?"

"I'm okay. Are you doing all right?" she gently asked.

My eyes started to fill up with tears. "I don't know. I feel ridiculous. Just being in this space is doing something to me." I felt as if I were reliving a memory that wasn't my own, knowing that the people who were killed had sat through a Bible study like we just had. "They welcomed this Dylann kid in to worship and study with them. And then they were murdered *in this room*. It's just too much. Do you think it's possible for a room to hold trauma? Because I feel it so deeply."

She nodded and took my hand in hers. After we sat in silence for a few minutes, we got up and thanked the pastor for leading during an incredibly difficult time. I glanced over at the aisle where a few of my teammates were chatting with the man who had sat behind me. They motioned us over.

"Jenny and Ashlee, meet Richard. He is a reporter with the *New York Times*. He's here as part of a larger story on how the community is showing up for the church and the ways they are pursuing healing."

I felt my cheeks warm as I wondered what Richard thought of my security rotations. There was no gunman, no manifesto, just a journalist with his notes.

Later, we met a small circle of women who were regulars of the Bible study.

One woman said she and her daughter had been there the night of the shooting. "I was in the back office, and when I heard gunshots we got real quiet, praying that the gunman wouldn't notice the light on or the door open. Thank God he didn't. But it's been so hard on my six-year-old, losing her dad the way she did. We both still have so many nightmares."

The older woman standing next to her gave her a warm side hug, then said, "I was supposed to be there that night. My friend even called me that day and encouraged me to come. I told her I couldn't make it but I would be there next week." She fought back tears. "I have so much guilt for even being alive. I miss my friends. Very much." Then she excused herself.

I watched her walk away from the circle of women. I imagined what the Bible study had meant to her over the years, the ways those in that room had prayed and checked in on each other, the ways they had celebrated when prayers were answered and maybe the ways they had held each other when they weren't. The ways they had become a community.

For these survivors to worship at Mother Emanuel was also to revisit a crime scene, a sacred space forever haunted with the image of a violent White gunman taking the lives of nine of their own.

● ● ●

Back at the hotel I fell onto my bed, exhausted. As I lay on top of the scratchy twin comforter, I reviewed the past forty-eight hours. I had stood next to a tree that was the site of indescribable violence and trauma for Black bodies and souls at the hands of White people. I had listened to plantation tour guides share the facts of their families' history with an "it is what it is" posture. I walked through markets that now sold wooden toys and Christmas ornaments and souvenirs in a building that used to sell human beings, with nary a plaque or acknowledgment of such history in sight. I read archived newspaper ads that told of the going rate to buy a Black baby, a Black teenager, a Black mother, a Black grandmother. I stood next to my friend as she took in how much she would have been worth, down to the dollar. I rode a carriage along the water next to beautiful, historic, colorful mansions—knowing full well that the only color those mansion owners loved was that which was painted on their walls, not the color of their fellow man. That the only way they paid for such pretty things was through the profits of another human's labor, another human's exploitation, another human's humiliation, another human's dehumanization.

I had heard from survivors of present-day lynchings that occurred inside their own house of worship, now forever haunted. I sat in city council meetings hearing about the disproportionate rate of homelessness among Black men, women, and families. I ate with Black police officers who provided for their families and were overwhelmed by a system that would not change. I looked at an empty lot behind a pawn shop where Walter Scott ran from a police officer who was both racist and perhaps too tired to do anything more than take aim, shoot, and lie.

I couldn't help but compare this trip to the one I had taken in college. In many ways, my time on Sankofa left me feeling as if I had dug up a time capsule, its racist contents buried and contained.

This trip, there was no time capsule, just the realization that since our country's inception, crime scene tape should cover every inch of America's land.

8

THE VERDICT

*Our anger is not about bitterness or hatred. It is about the desire
for equality and justice. It's about wanting racism to end. We're
tired of suffering and want to know what equality, dignity and
respect feel like before we die. . . . Our anger is justified and
Whites should be as angry about these injustices as we are. We're
frustrated that they are not. If they were, things would change.*

POCAHONTAS GERTLER

JULY 14, 2013, WAS A SUNDAY. The evening prior, the verdict for
the murder of Trayvon Martin—a seventeen-year-old Black boy who
loved airplanes and dreamt of being a pilot, killed at the hands of George
Zimmerman, a neighborhood watch member in Trayvon's community—
was announced. Zimmerman was found not guilty of second-degree
murder after a jury heard three weeks of testimony. The verdict was
highly anticipated by many, including those on the diversity team
and myself.

That Sunday morning, I was working backstage at the church when
one of the worship leaders invited me to the back office. This was not a
casual invite. I was rarely included in these meetings, but the senior
pastor wanted to meet with the diversity team to process and plan our
response to the verdict.

We walked into the office, where I found other members of the team
already there. I quickly glanced around the room to see who else was

invited. The worship leader sat next to a few musicians from the band, across from the executive producer and the technical director. At the center of it all was the senior pastor. The conversation was already underway as I was encouraged to squeeze in.

"With all due respect, I am hurting badly," one of our musicians said, "and to not have anything said to pastor or comfort me, or to simply acknowledge me and the rest of the Black community this morning publicly, feels incredibly painful." He turned his face from the direction of the senior pastor, took off his glasses, and rubbed his eyes.

"This news is so new. I am not at my best when I am reacting to something off the cuff," the senior pastor began in response. "We don't have enough information yet. Let's wait for other pastors to make their statements in their churches this morning first, and let us learn from any mistakes for when we respond."

"But we don't need those pastors' words; your church needs your words to shepherd them now," the same musician responded.

The door opened, and Austin and that weekend's guest pastor, Judy, tiptoed into the room; their faces showed they had no idea what they had just walked into.

"I feel like I'm disappointing you all," the pastor finally said. Several people nodded reluctantly while some shed silent tears. "Please be patient with me. I just need some more time."

A prayer was offered from somebody for wisdom and patience, along with comfort for Trayvon's family. "Amen," we all agreed as the prayer and meeting came to a close. People started to move about the room as I lingered in my seat.

I had sat quietly through the whole meeting, unsure what else could be said to change the pastor's mind. I did not push back or threaten to resign if he didn't say something. In that instant, I didn't understand that his response, which felt like an isolated occurrence, was actually as common and predictable as the sun's arrival that morning. And then the weekend continued as planned.

Until it didn't.

During her sermon, Judy made one comment to subtly address the pain in the room regarding the verdict. Word soon spread that she had gone against the senior pastor's directive to her not to speak to the verdict. Now, church staff who had invited her were being told their jobs—and the likelihood that Judy would be asked back to preach—were in jeopardy.

Anecdotes like that began to spread, and over the next few weeks and months, I reflected on the senior pastor's promises the week that Trayvon Martin was killed to say something once there was a verdict, once we "knew all the facts." I learned that the musician who pushed back at the meeting was often told by the senior pastor he was at risk of becoming a "one-trick pony" known only for his continued advocacy for racial justice. I learned that Austin realized her job was likely at risk once the senior pastor started apologizing to a group of unsatisfied people—those she was directly educating and inspiring about what real racial justice should be. She was so successful at her job that she pushed us past the line, one that our leaders weren't willing to cross with us.

Was my church guilty of being led by what Martin Luther King Jr. described as a group of "White moderates"? If so, was I guilty of following them?

I went directly to King's famous "Letter from Birmingham Jail" to look for evidence, comparing what he wrote with what I had heard from the leaders of the church.

King began: "I must confess that over the last few years I have been gravely disappointed with the White moderate. I have almost reached the regrettable conclusion that the Negro's great stumbling block in the stride toward freedom is not the White Citizen's Council-er or the Ku Klux Klanner, but the White moderate who is more devoted to "order" than to justice . . ."

What I had heard from leaders of the church: *We have to go a few yards at a time. This is too important to risk a hail Mary play. And we must do things in accordance with our culture of "excellence" so no one can critique or argue with us.*

Dr. King continued: " . . . who prefers a negative peace which is the absence of tension to a positive peace which is the presence of justice . . ."

I was hearing: *We want to avoid rocking the boat in any way that might be unpopular with White donors and board members and lead to angry emails from White congregants.*

Dr. King: " . . . who constantly says 'I agree with you in the goal you seek, but I can't agree with your methods of direct action . . .'"

Leaders: *Let's stay quiet and avoid being labeled "political" or "divisive."*

Dr. King: ". . . who paternalistically feels he can set the timetable for another man's freedom, who lives by the myth of time and who constantly advises the Negro to wait until a 'more convenient season.'"

Leaders: *If we rush things, there will be many White people not yet onboard and we just want as many of them to come with us as possible,* and *I promise you, when this person leaves I will replace them with a person of color,* and *I'm hearing from so many people about so many issues. It's not fair for me to only speak about this one.*

Dr. King: "Shallow understanding from people of goodwill is more frustrating than absolute misunderstanding from people of ill will. Lukewarm acceptance is much more bewildering than outright rejection."

Another verdict was in—I was being led by White moderates at their pace. It felt dizzyingly clarifying. It also felt, to use King's words, bewildering.

Because I, too, was guilty of following the leader of our church. I trusted that he had been at this work longer than I had and therefore had a more mature perspective, that eventually the pace would change and his "second conversion," or change of heart he often referenced when the topic of race came up, would lead to a deeper sense of urgency toward justice. I was following him also because I truly believed a church that prided itself on being influential could make a real difference in the larger church's approach to achieving justice. I felt duped.

During that Sunday office meeting, the pastor's reasoning felt famil-iar. It was an argument I had heard so often throughout my time at the organization that I came to believe it myself: this issue of racial justice was too big of a thing to "get wrong." But when I examined the logic from that day, I kept coming back to the all-important question that I learned from racial justice leader Brenda Salter McNeil: "On whose terms?" On whose terms do we decide what is right or wrong? And on whose timeline?

I sat with that question for a bit and soon realized that silence was getting it wrong. Waiting was getting it wrong. Asking Black men and women to lead others in worship in a church where they did not experi-ence pastoral care in times of fear and pain and sadness was getting it wrong. Not being a consistent example for other churches in our com-mitment to racial justice was getting it wrong. There was no such thing as a perfect response, but there was such a thing as a just one.

I believe that the senior pastor was deeply afraid. I imagine he felt torn in that moment, trying to find a way to appease everyone. But he seemed more afraid of the potential backlash from White people in his congregation than the real, upfront feedback from Black people on his staff who he claimed to be friends with and did ministry alongside. He was afraid of not doing it perfectly, so he did nothing at all. Except it wasn't nothing. His inaction was a powerful act of centering his own comfort, his own timeline, and his own agenda over what justice required of him in that moment.

This pastor was not the first to respond in this way. In the book of Luke, Jesus was dining on the Sabbath with a group of religious experts. A very ill man was seated nearby when Jesus asked the group whether a healing would be lawful on that day or not. They remained silent. So after healing the man, Jesus addressed them again: "Which of you, hav-ing a son or an ox that has fallen into a well on a Sabbath day, will not immediately pull him out?" (Luke 14:5). They again chose to stay silent.

Jesus was dealing with very devout Jews. These religious experts were not evil—they loved the Lord and wanted to be faithful to him. In knowing and keeping the laws, they believed they were doing just that. But that's not always how it works in God's kingdom.

The religious leaders here sound a lot like the original White moderates. Jesus clearly saw their desire for not only order but control.

Maybe this is one of the reasons Martin Luther King Jr. called out the White moderates. Maybe he knew that obvious displays of racism would later evolve into less overt (yet still incredibly dangerous and real) forms of racism. And if he was having difficulty moving, motivating, and gaining momentum during the time of Jim Crow laws, segregated water fountains and schools and swimming pools, blatant voter suppression, and beyond, he must have known that one day—when those barriers were crossed and oppression no longer was a sign that said "colored" and "Whites"—he would hear the tired "Look how far we've come" line.

To most White people, White moderates appear reasonable, logical, and wise. There is often an awareness of the issues and injustices that invites trust and conveys authority. But when awareness is not coupled with action on the terms of the people most negatively impacted by the injustice, what good is it really? Who and what does it ultimately serve?

If I wanted to make sure I was not keeping pace with a White moderate, I would have to stop following one.

The murder of Trayvon Martin got the attention of many White people and even led some to wake up and pay closer attention. The aftermath of the Zimmerman verdict reoriented me. It led me to more deeply understand my own commitment to stop doing nothing. And not just on my terms.

9

A CONFESSION

It is hard to get it across to you since you've picked up this bad habit of not listening. By this time you ought to be teachers yourselves, yet here I find you need someone to sit down with you and go over the basics on God again, starting from square one—baby's milk, when you should have been on solid food long ago! Milk is for beginners, inexperienced in God's ways; solid food is for the mature, who have some practice in telling right from wrong.

HEBREWS 5:11-14 (*THE MESSAGE*)

Lament recognizes the struggles of life and cries out for justice against existing injustices. The status quo is not to be celebrated but instead must be challenged.

SOONG-CHAN RAH

While I was growing up, my dad was always the first to adopt new technology. My babysitters loved watching me because our family was the first in the neighborhood to have AOL dial-up and instant messenger. He was loyal to all things Apple, even sporting a jacket and nylon briefcase with the famous logo before it was a household name. Basically, my dad was a cooler version of the science-experiment obsessed dad played by Rick Moranis in the '90s movie *Honey I Shrunk the Kids*. It was no surprise that when the latest in video technology came out, he was all in. We somehow ended up with four laserdisc players. He used them for his media company, but we had a few backups in the house. There were a few movies I played most often: *The Sound of Music, The Wizard of Oz,* and (because this was the 1980s, after all) *Amy Grant: In Concert—Age to Age Tour.*

Amy Grant was the "it" girl of Contemporary Christian Music (or CCM as the church kids called it). I was born the year of *Age to Age's* recording and felt a deep connection to Amy and the music. Watching her on TV almost became an extension of church.

My small hands would run along the stack of laserdiscs filed in the wooden cabinet of the family room's entertainment center. When I found the right one, I would pull it from its giant sleeve, careful not to leave any smudges that would cause the disc to skip.

The opening number was an acapella trio singing "I Have Decided to Follow Jesus." Amy would make her way to the stage in an oversized cardigan with her big hair held in place by barrettes, and I would settle in, ready to sing along.

I knew all the songs by heart, but there was one that always stayed stuck in my head, its lyrics and Andrews Sisters–style tune so catchy I would find myself humming it long after the song ended. It was called "Fat Baby" and began, "I know a man, maybe you know him, too. You never can tell; he might even be you."

This man, who was only concerned with being saved but not with growing in his faith, was filling up on milk instead of moving on to real food. The song made a jab at his stomach for not being able to handle solid foods, meaning he was at risk of staying a "fat baby" forever. (This did not age well, friends.)

As Amy and her backup singers danced around the stage, I would giggle, imagining a grown man dressed up in a big diaper, wanting only milk from his bottle. This poor baby didn't know what he was missing out on.

Now I wondered if most people realized they were being fed a diet like this. What had I been missing out on? And what did I have in common with this baby? As I sat in the aftermath of the Zimmerman verdict, I reflected on my current spiritual diet, what I had been fed, and what had been missing. What began as an inventory quickly turned into a time for reflection, which led to lament and, ultimately, confession.

I lament actual human lives being taken, shortened, stolen, and brutally destroyed. I lament the frequency and the fear experienced within Black communities especially. I lament the way racism robs people of their dignity and humanity.

I lament that the White church mostly avoids a robust diet and instead serves only skim milk, thinking that will be enough to satisfy one's appetite. I lament that most White American churches feast on a skim gospel.

I lament the wasted opportunities for discipleship and transformation from the gospel—the full gospel, not the gospel according to White moderate–approved Jesus.

I lament that many civil rights activists' words have been used not to challenge and correct, but to comfort and reassure that most of the hard work is behind us and that we are the "good ones" for even talking about "these issues" at all. I lament that we skim over the hard parts and experience a sense of false unity as we stand and sing "We Shall Overcome" together, as if singing in unison is all that it will take. As if we can easily replace the word "shall" for "have."

I lament days when social media feeds are filled with Chicken Soup for the Soul–style quotes and gratitude toward Dr. King, as if, as Andre Henry said, "he gave the 'I Have a Dream' speech and then ascended to heaven" rather than being so hated that he was relentlessly threatened and ultimately murdered for his work to make his dream come true.

I lament seeking reconciliation instead of justice, believing for so long that reconciliation could resolve all injustices. The more I reflect, the more I see that true reconciliation is a result of justice.

I lament the years I spent earnestly drinking from that cup and the many ways it leaves me feeling cheated, as today I am nearly gorging myself on more wholistic ideas and richer stories that were kept hidden.

I repent of believing that we were doing enough because "at least we weren't ignoring racism completely."

I repent of times I said or did nothing in the face of ignorance, racist remarks hidden behind "it's just a joke," and the perpetuation of stereotypes.

I repent of trusting timelines and rationales and excuses that obstructed true discipleship, true justice, and opportunities for the beginning of healing and reconciliation.

I repent of times when I worked alongside Black and Brown friends, convinced that if we just showed the White people in the room their scars, their fresh wounds, and their pain that eyes would be opened, hearts and minds convinced.

I repent of thinking White people were the answer or that the goal was my own understanding.

I repent of when I thought I was one of the "good White people," when I looked down on other White people who weren't yet where I prided myself at being, when I expected people of color to be grateful for my commitment to the work.

I repent of thinking this list will ever come to an end, that the work will ever be finished, that I won't be adding things for the rest of my life.

Whiteness might have offered a skim gospel to me, but I am the one who drank it.

Forgive me. For what I have done and for what I have left undone.

I was drinking a watered-down gospel for so long that when I started really drinking from Jesus' words and beliefs, the whole gospel became overwhelming in its richness.

10

HANGING BY A THREAD

*Maybe my understanding of the Good News of Jesus is not
actually Jesus' understanding of the Good News.*

LISA SHARON HARPER

Break up with White Jesus.

ANDRE HENRY

ONE DEFINITION OF REPENTANCE IS TO STOP WALKING in the
direction you were headed and turn around. A 180-degree turn allows
you to move *away* from something and *toward* something else. I could
no longer keep walking toward what I now recognized as a watered-
down gospel and a Whitewashed faith. As I made the painful departure
from people and places and a job that I loved, I kept the words of Maya
Angelou on a loop in my mind: "When someone shows you who they are,
believe them the first time."

For all the years of my life, the White American church had been
consistent. At times it had shown signs of change, growth, and inclusion, but its growth had limits, and it almost always returned to its
original ways. It had been telling me over and over again who it was. I
had just refused to accept it, holding on to hope for change. It was like
the church was a brick wall and I kept running hard into it, pushing for
breakthrough. But the wall did not budge even as I stood bloodied,

bruised, and exhausted. It was time to walk away. Coming to terms with this was painful. In many ways, it felt like my faith was hanging by a thread.

Like anyone who has gone through a traumatic loss knows, I spent much time mulling over details and memories from the past—searching for clues along the way that hinted at where I was today. One memory in particular kept rising to the surface.

●   ●   ●

Just after my husband, John, and I were married and before I took the job at the megachurch, two friends from college invited us to their new church. It had recently been revitalized under the new leadership of two White men who had roots in social work and social justice. The church sat at the corner of a classic Chicago North Side street, its beige exterior popping against the bright red door that led into the sanctuary. It was a beautiful but not an especially ornate building, with stained-glass windows along the south side and Jesus depicted in stained glass at the center of the east wall. Inside, hanging in front of the stained-glass Jesus were six more laminated art prints, each one of Jesus depicted as a Black or Brown man. They moved slightly as they dangled by a thin, clear string from the ceiling.

I was immediately curious. I knew historically Jesus was Brown, of Middle Eastern descent, and Jewish, and yet I could not recall ever seeing Jesus depicted as anything but White. John and I greatly appreciated over the following Sundays that the pastors regularly shared ideas in their sermons from Black theologians and thinkers, Indigenous activists, and Latinx and Asian leaders. Those ideas shaped not only the message but also the culture of the church, and we became inspired by a Christian theology deeply concerned and involved with injustices of the world. "For God's glory and neighbor's good" was at the center of the church's call. The pastors pulled from their training in social work and theology to point us to this call again and again. My understanding of the gospel began to shift. If it wasn't good news for all my neighbors, maybe it wasn't actually good news.

We began throwing ourselves into the life of the church. We volunteered in the nursery, joined a small group, and helped with the church's garden. We planned events; attended protests related to racial, social, and environmental injustices; and advocated for policies related to homelessness with local officials in Chicago, as nearly 60 percent of those served in the homeless service system are Black.

That racial disparity was apparent in our church's warming center, a weekly gathering place where people experiencing homelessness could come to the church basement for a shower, a hot meal, clothes, and a bagged lunch for the next day.

One Sunday, the pastor's wife, a sociology professor, announced she would be leading a book club on *Divided by Faith: Evangelical Religion and the Problem of Race in America*. John and I signed up before we left the building. A few weeks later we met in their apartment for the first time—about fifteen of us crammed on couches and folding chairs to make room. *Divided By Faith* thoroughly examined why Martin Luther King Jr.'s quote about Sunday morning being the most segregated hour of the week was not only true when he said it in the 1960s but was still true today. Our church certainly fit that narrative, as we were mostly White and twenty-somethings.

I raised my own concern at one of our first book club gatherings. "Should we be worried that we are lacking diversity in our congregation? It doesn't seem to line up with our values around racial reconciliation." I paused, wanting to make sure I was making my point clear. "One of the first things I noticed about this church was the intentionality to address racism, to embrace and uplift the Black and Brown experience. We are not hiding it. It's in the messages and in the work in the community. And our beliefs are quite literally hanging up in the sanctuary."

"Are they, though?" interjected Rick, a member of the church and honestly one of the smartest people I had ever met. He was getting his PhD at the University of Chicago, and when he spoke, which wasn't often, I was inclined to listen.

"Those Jesus images have all been added recently," Rick said. "It would take very little effort to cut those strings down, to remove any physical evidence that they were ever there."

I pictured the sanctuary: the Black and Brown Jesuses hanging in the foreground, the White Jesus in the background, his light-skinned face, fair hair, and pale body literally a part of the church building. White Jesus' presence was so integral to the design that removal would take real effort and result in real brokenness. His absence would not only be noticed but felt as the cool outside air entered in through the shards of shattered glass, while noises from outside would mingle with the sounds of our worship.

Conversely, the visual representation of any non-White Jesus was literally hanging by a thread.

$$\bullet \quad \bullet \quad \bullet$$

Looking back, I was naive to think that having a few more people of color in attendance would alone fix the segregated hour on Sunday mornings. Getting Black and Brown folks to leave their churches and fill our pews in order to diversify our church would not mean we were no longer a divided body.

Like many things Martin Luther King Jr. said or wrote that are reduced to a quote, the heart of his message often gets diluted or diverted. His interview on "Meet the Press" where he famously lamented 11 a.m. on Sunday as "the most segregated hour in Christian America" is often at the forefront of discussions around the desire for diversity. But what if we had been trying to fix the wrong problem? What if Reverend King had noticed a different problem altogether?

"What deeply troubles me now," he shared with close friends, "is that for all the steps we've taken toward integration, I've come to believe that we are integrating into a burning house."

Was desegregating the church simply inviting us all to a burning building? And was following White Jesus leading us to the same place?

As I looked around at the larger American church, I discovered the undeniable reality that we weren't just divided by our place of worship at that infamous 11 a.m. Sunday hour; we were divided by our practicing very different faiths altogether.

Our kingdoms "on earth as it is in heaven" looked different and were even starkly opposed—maybe because two different Jesuses were being worshiped on the throne.

White Jesus' kingdom involved great concern for the individual, freedom, power, success, and order. Black and Brown Jesus understood a life of oppression because he lived it. White Jesus kept his circle exclusive and elite, only inviting in those who could be an asset to his ministry and his agenda. Black and Brown Jesus stood with the outcast, the downtrodden, the marginalized, and the one excluded from the table. White Jesus held a scarcity mindset, deeply rooted in fear. Black and Brown Jesus offered abundance. White Jesus was a mascot. Black and Brown Jesus was a freedom fighter and a Savior.

"The Jesus that Black folks worship doesn't ask questions like, 'But does the gospel really have anything to do with race and justice?'" I often heard Austin say.

As I reflected on her words, the artwork in the church that hung from a string flashed in my mind. In one image, Jesus was a Middle Eastern man trapped behind barbed wire; in another, Jesus was a Black man with a crown of thorns atop his head as blood ran down the gashes in his face. Jesus was not only near the oppressed—he was an embodiment of them.

All this time, I had thought fighting racism in the church and beyond was about awareness and education, about convincing and pleading, about changing the hearts and minds of those in White Christian spaces. I thought we could just add Black and Brown Jesus to the teachings of White Jesus, that somehow our faith could hold both, but the container of White Jesus does not allow for this. White Jesus dilutes and rejects anything that challenges its supremacy.

I thought the work was to change White Jesus, but the truth is, White Jesus cannot be changed. Instead, the work is to turn and follow Jesus with brown skin, Jesus the Middle Eastern Jew, Jesus the refugee, Jesus the divider, Jesus the disrupter, Jesus the falsely accused, Jesus the arrested, Jesus the executed. Jesus, the way out of the desert and into abundant life.

I don't know if we'll ever be able to eliminate White Jesus, but we can choose not to follow him. We can repent, turn from White Jesus, and run toward the kingdom with Black and Brown Jesus on the throne. We might have a hard time recognizing him at first. We might have to wrestle with why we've resisted following him for so long and come to terms with our fears of where he's going to take us. He might lead us to places we aren't ready to go, both inside ourselves and out in the world. And he most likely will turn our entire world upside down.

I can't say where this path will take you, but I can tell you that once I walked away from White Jesus, I never looked back.

11

AMAZING GRACE

True belonging is not passive. It's not the belonging that comes with just joining a group. It's not fitting in or pretending or selling out because it's safer. It's a practice that requires us to be vulnerable, get uncomfortable, and learn how to be present.

BRENÉ BROWN

If you have come here to help me you are wasting your time, but if you have come because your liberation is bound up with mine, then let us work together.

LILLA WATSON

MY REPENTANCE WORK MEANT I was turning away from a lot, including the idea that racial justice work should be confined to the church. I had put so much work, so much trust, so much hope in the church and then in one meeting, it was essentially gone. I was moving toward a wider vision of racial justice that could dwell everywhere. This redirection didn't mean I no longer cared about my faith; it meant I cared about it more. As I worked more closely with people from marginalized communities, I found as Kaitlin Curtice, author of *Native*, wrote, "the margins as holy places. The world turned upside down."

Judy, the guest pastor, spoke up the weekend of the George Zimmerman verdict because she was following Black and Brown Jesus: the Jesus of the marginalized. She later told me that not only were people from the community she pastored sitting in the service—people who were reeling from the verdict and in need of her pastoral voice—but that she also ran into one of the musicians, a friend and Black man, backstage that morning. "The world doesn't care about Black men," he had said, his voice tired and his eyes puffy and red from crying. She gave him a hug and spoke her truth back to him: "It's not the whole world that doesn't care about Black men, just some of the world."

Knowing that musician was part of what made her do something that day. She wasn't focused on convincing White people to do something differently or making them feel guilty or ignorant. She set her sights on making sure that the Black man she hugged, who was raising his own Black sons, was seen by her and given the importance and acknowledgment that moment required.

As we reminisced about that day, she asked me if I thought the senior pastor had been changed by knowing that Black musician. "Isn't that why he always encourages everyone to widen their social circles? So that we can be transformed by knowing and being known? So that we can be bold enough to love well? But how can we love well if we don't know well?"

She had a way of preaching that could not be contained, even over a phone call.

I sat in my living room long after our call ended, pondering those questions. They were surprisingly simple. How had my relationships with people, specifically people of color, changed and challenged me? How did knowing them not just confirm what I thought I knew, but instead lead me to listen, give space for and submit to their experiences, especially if they were unlike my own?

I thought way back to my first encounter with Katrina, my Sankofa partner, when she told me about being bullied about her hair at a sleepover. What would have happened if I had jumped in and said, "I was made fun of in elementary school too"? We often build from shared experiences to create connections so that, when we come to the parts of our stories that are different, we still have something to stand on. But what if when we get to those parts that are different, one of us is still looking for similarities? *You were teased? I was teased! You felt left out in middle school? Me too! Your grandparents didn't go to college? Neither did mine! Life was hard? Life was hard!*

We have gotten so good at finding common ground that we have little practice at what to do when a person's experience confuses us or is one we haven't had.

It's not a problem of finding enough in common. It's an issue of getting curious about what we don't have in common and then believing those differences are real.

I believe that was a hinge point in my relationship with Katrina (and in every relationship with friends of color). Were I not present to her pain, not letting it take up all the space, I don't know if she would have continued to share, trust, and walk with me. If I hadn't told myself, *Jenny, your story has been told and it's time to listen to another story*, I don't know if I would have had that moment of awakening on the bus.

It wasn't all about me. And it wasn't only about them. It was about us, belonging to each other and to ourselves. The more I came back to that idea, the more I knew it to be true. Writer and activist Audre Lorde laid it out quite simply when she said, "I am not free while any woman is unfree, even if her shackles are very different from my own."

If *we* made it, *I* made it. In that order.

● ● ●

"I can't do the work of reconciliation all by myself," Austin would often say to me, smiling, when we worked together at the church. She said it because it was true, but I'm pretty sure she knew I struggled with feeling qualified or equipped, with desperately wanting to get this work right, with knowing enough to take my own actions seriously. We were in a work environment where there was a hierarchy to who we learned from—leadership wanted the leading expert, the scholar, the one who you could easily identify as a credible source.

When we first started our work together and Austin asked me to lead part of a training or workshop, my instinct was to say no, to help her find someone more qualified. I once suggested another teammate, a White woman who had six biracial adopted brothers and sisters. I flashed back to the day we all were introduced to each other, how I was a tiny bit jealous at the credibility of her reason for belonging to the diversity group. I usually fumbled my way through my own answer, not knowing how far back to go and what would easily explain my presence, as though my desire for justice needed an alibi.

"Don't you think she would do a better job?" I asked sincerely as we dried our hands in the office bathroom.

She turned her head from looking at my reflection in the mirror to facing me eye-to-eye. "Jenny, if I have to wait for every White person to have a bunch of biracial adopted siblings before they can do anything about racism, I'm going to be waiting forever. We don't have that kind of time, love."

Austin didn't recoil from my excuses; she moved toward them and challenged me. She was not soft nor did she go easy on me. Because of her, I was often able to adjust my understanding for who or what needed to be the focus in order to pursue racial justice. It was rarely the White person among us. Yet there were still times when I was caught up with myself, in the trappings of perfection and shame that were just a distraction from the real work at hand. I was worried the low hum in my head, that said, *You don't deserve any of this. Not the friendships, not the ability to join in on the work as a White woman, not a seat at the table,* would be heard by others if I didn't get it right every time.

She graciously pushed me past my point of comfort. I wanted to be fully ready, to know everything I needed to know, to have arrived at "expert White person pursuing racial justice" status. But deep down, I was scared out of my mind—scared especially of making mistakes I wasn't able to see on my own due to years of unchallenged blind spots. If someone pointed those errors out, wouldn't my team be so disappointed that they had backed the girl who was still constantly discovering how much she didn't know, and that what she once thought was airtight capital T truth was riddled with holes?

When Austin called me about an idea she had for an upcoming video web-series called "The Next Question," she said those words again: "I can't do this work by myself." Her vision was to create a visual space for Black women to be heard and seen. Tired of where conversations on racism often stalled out, Austin wanted conversations that were fueled by curiosity, imagination, humanity, and unapologetic boldness. "We have all these brilliant minds that we can ask anything of," Austin said, "so why am I hearing interviews with Michelle Alexander asking her to explain what the old Jim Crow was, when the title of her book is *The New Jim Crow*? What a waste!" Austin wanted to help us get deeper—to get to the next questions that would allow us to meaningfully learn, grow, and engage with issues of racism and injustice, and to see the guests on the show as whole, full people. I said yes immediately. We had worked together on video projects in the past, so I wasn't all that surprised that we would be dreaming about this new project together. I was, however, very surprised when she asked me to be one of her two cohosts.

On the first day of filming, as Austin, our other cohost, Chi Chi (a Black woman we had both worked with at the church), and I changed in the basement of the home we were using as our studio, we talked quickly about the day's guest. My heart pounded as we steamed skirts and shirts and as I put on another layer of deodorant. The home did not have air conditioning, and we were filming on a humid early June afternoon in Chicago. I was thankful for the coolness of the basement and a bit of reprieve from the heat.

Upstairs as the film crew made last-minute lighting adjustments, we were delighted by the accidental cohesion in our wardrobe. I had picked out a gray T-shirt with a red heart across the chest surrounding the words "Midwest is best." Our guest for the day was Iowa native, *New York Times* journalist, MacArthur Genius award recipient, and soon-to-be Pulitzer Prize–winner Nikole Hannah-Jones. I had listened to hours of interviews with Nikole prior to this day and read as much as I could get my hands on. I was mentally prepared for the conversation. Emotionally I was in my head about the rules I would follow: never interrupt, let the other women go first, and don't take up too much space. I was hyperaware that I was the only White woman on the show, which would be the case for most of our episodes. I felt I had a responsibility to model why I was there. I planned on erring on the side of being seen but not heard.

At least, that was my plan until I spoke it out loud. Austin kept steaming her black-and-white-striped blouse and said, slowly and very casually, "I'm gonna need for you to say something, JP."

I nodded, frustrated with myself that I needed that permission yet again just minutes away from being mic'd up, frustrated that my focus on how I appeared meant my two Black cohosts would be forced to take on the weight of the work while I sat there minding my manners, following rules no one had asked me to adhere to.

Nikole was obviously brilliant. She rattled off dates and facts with ease, and I was blown away by how much we all learned. We made each other laugh, which was one of our main goals. I'm sure the bourbon we drank as we filmed didn't hurt. And I said things nervously and imperfectly. But I showed up.

When the episode was released a few months later, a White coworker mentioned how much she was enjoying the show. "I think you are so brave for being there. I could never do that. I would be so scared."

I knew she was implying that part of my bravery was being the only White woman in that space talking to Black women about the disparities in education, prison, police brutality, and every other nook and cranny of society. I thanked her for watching and said I thought it was actually much braver of them to invite me and share experiences and fears that demonstrated their willingness to trust me and believe in the space we were creating together.

As if I was there because of anything but their grace. As if the work was about proving myself to be a "good one." As if, on a larger scale, any

White person could show up to this work of pursuing racial justice with a chance at doing it perfectly, flawlessly, and impressively.

"The best criticism of the bad is the practice of the better," wrote Franciscan priest and author Richard Rohr in his book *Things Hidden: Scripture as Spirituality*. The invitation to racial justice work wasn't rocket science; it was actually very clear. It was the practice of the better, of vulnerability, of discomfort, of belief, of presence. I had often made it much more complicated than it needed to be. I was not invited to partner with my friends in this work because I was good or exceptional; I was there because I believed them when they said, "This is my experience" even when that experience did not match my own. When you shift who you believe, it changes who and what you don't. Everything changes. I was there because believing them meant I was being transformed and letting things go that did not serve us both. But mostly I was there because of love and amazing grace, with a clear and imperfect path toward practicing the better. I was learning to belong to myself, and mostly, to belong to a larger *us*.

12

DEAR SON

January 2015

Dear Elliot,

My darling boy. I knew for a long time that I wanted to be a mom, but I never knew how much I would love being *your* mom. Almost five months in, I can already tell how sweet and silly and thoughtful and interested in the world you are.

I was in labor for over sixty hours, and when you were finally born, I was exhausted in every way possible. There are two moments I won't ever forget that occurred immediately after you were born: hearing your dad announce, "It's a boy!" (which I had been pretty convinced of, even though we hadn't found out beforehand) and the midwife telling me how beautiful the color of your skin was.

You were born on August 18, 2014, the same day that the National Guard arrived in Ferguson, Missouri. Just nine days earlier, an eighteen-year-old Black son and recent high school graduate was shot and killed by a White police officer there. While we were counting your fingers and toes, protestors were on the ground chanting, "Hands up, don't shoot." Although August of 2014 made me a mother, another mother eight hours away was grieving, robbed of watching her own son continue to grow up. That mom was added to a club of Black parents that I'm sure she never wanted to belong to.

I remember your dad and I sitting in our hospital room that night, feeling shaken back into reality and saddened that this was the state of the world we were bringing you into—a world infected with so much hatred and anger and fear. We spent the first night of your life talking about how something really big was happening in Ferguson, and at the same time, something really tiny and delicate had just happened in our Chicago hospital room to grow our family.

I kept thinking about what the midwife had said to me about your skin color and wondered if all moms hear that—and even if they do, at what moment did their son's skin color shift from being beautiful to being a worry.

Darling boy, I have so many fears and hopes for you. I am afraid that, as a White male, you won't think the topics of racism and justice apply to you. That you will think you are exempt or that, as long as you don't spew hatred, you are not part of the problem. I fear that you won't work to share and ultimately eliminate the privileges you have been given, that the lens through which you see and understand the world will be stained by stereotypes and supremacy, and that you will not choose to push back against these lies. I am scared you will grow resentful of learning about the many problems created and perpetuated by White men, that knowing the fuller story of history will make you defensive and hardened.

I hope that you are a lifelong learner, that you stay curious, ask lots of questions, and see the journey of justice and reconciliation as an irresistible voyage, a gift to your future and never a threat. My prayers are filled with a deep longing that you discover a strong sense of self and that you join others who are vigilantly kicking down ladders that have only propped up boys with the same amount of melanin in their skin as you.

I am committed to expanding your world, and I long for moments when people of different backgrounds and cultures from your own share perspectives you don't know, and that you have courage to seek to understand their stories and to be a humble and sincere listener. I hope that you are stretched to hold tight to both the beauty and the pain that are sure to emerge for you as a co-conspirator. I hope for endurance and for a community that challenges you and reminds you that you are not alone in your attempts to be a voice alongside those whose voices are so often ignored.

So many people ask what the "something" is that they should do. But I pray that you will not just *do* something but, like Dr. King said, *be* the something that helps bring healing and grace and justice into our world. May you embody this work, and may your life be an act of rebellion against places and systems that exclude and perpetuate inequality.

Love always,

Mama

13

RAISING WHITE PARENTS

They always say time changes things, but you
actually have to change them yourself.

ANDY WARHOL

AFTER I HAD ELLIOT, I was surprised by how many people casually commented on the hope he brought them—a hope founded on the idea that this child was being brought up in a more welcoming, tolerant world. They said things like, "Our country is being led by its first Black president," and "Elliot's classmates will be from such diverse ethnic backgrounds. Every time I drive by the schools around here, they are all playing together!"

The first few times comments like these came my way, I was caught off guard. I was coming out of the fog of postpartum and reading Ta-Nehisi Coates' *Atlantic* article "The Case for Reparations." His opening lines alone are incredibly heavy: "Two hundred fifty years of slavery. Ninety years of Jim Crow. Sixty years of separate but equal. Thirty-five years of racist housing policy. Until we reckon with our compounding moral debts, America will never be whole." I was also watching footage of military tanks lining the streets of Ferguson, Missouri, after the murder of recent high school graduate Michael Brown by police. I had grown wary of equating any sort of diversity with the inevitability of justice, and I was wary of any mindset that discouraged a sense of urgency. Also, I was having a hard time being hopeful about the inevitability of progress, the belief that *of course it will be better for our kids than it was for us*—as if injustice was like a rock in the stream being worn down over time no matter what. I supposed it was progress that the desire for justice was being named, but the naming was simply the starting line. And we weren't close to crossing any sort of finish line.

The antiracism work and learning I was doing in my own life quickly expanded to include preparing my kids to engage in their own work. I could not raise them to be the best versions of themselves without this being at the center of their hearts and souls. That understanding drove me and grounded my parenting. But it didn't all happen overnight.

In the summer of 2020 after Ahmaud Arbery, George Floyd, Breonna Taylor, and too many other Black men and women were murdered, so many people displayed a desire to do something—an urgency unlike anything I'd ever witnessed before. Quite literally overnight, the White gaze fell on not only the plight of injustices Black Americans faced but also our (White people's) own contributions to those injustices, what sort of legacy we were leaving, and what kind of training, if any, we were providing for our own children. Many White parents found ourselves with children watching, asking questions, and expecting us to have done some work to prepare them for a moment like this. And to be blunt, many of us were coming up way too short.

I was in the middle of attending a two-week class on raising antiracist kids when George Floyd was murdered. We met over Zoom one Thursday, and the following Monday, Memorial Day, the world seemed to have changed as news spread of his death. We met three days later, and I could feel the eagerness through the screen for the class to start. Our instructor mostly stayed true to her notes and slides, but the Q&A session almost exclusively addressed the question, "Do we talk to our young kids about what happened, and, if so, how?"

I personally started getting requests from acquaintances, friends, journalists, and churches to speak to questions like, "How do we talk to our kids about Black Lives Matter and George Floyd's murder and police violence?" and "What else should we be doing?" I was thrown by how quickly much of the focus went from "What should I be doing?" to "What should I be doing *so my children learn x, y, and z*?" I answered the questions as best I could, encouraging parents to not feel the need to lead their children to places they had never been themselves. In one interview, I answered by simply saying, "I think it's important to ask ourselves why we haven't been having these conversations with our kids before this. What has kept us silent? And what do we need to do to make this an ongoing, proactive part of our family culture?" I was encouraged by the earnest desire but also nervous that the passion and urgency would eventually fizzle out.

In an instant, countless White parents were drinking from a firehose of history and sociology, evaluating lifelong-held beliefs and assumptions while trying to teach their children. No wonder so many felt overwhelmed and, as a result, *stuck*.

● ● ●

A friend once told me that becoming a father made him feel like a first-generation logger. Apparently, it takes years and years, generations even, to yield enough trees to sustain a harvest. While others have metaphorical parenting fields filled with legacies and wisdom from previous generations, my friend began his parenthood experience looking at a mostly empty plot of land. What remained—rotted trees and weeds— represented addiction and abandonment. He had a choice to ignore the harm of the past or to spend his life clearing away those patterns and legacies he did not want to pass down. Once that hard work was done, he would be able to plant seeds in hopes that his children and their children's children would have something of worth left. He would never enjoy the feeling of inheriting a strong family legacy. But he had control over passing one on.

That image of an empty field always stayed with me. How many White parents were staring into their own fields realizing, for perhaps the first time, that what they thought was a full harvest was actually many harmful trees that needed to be cut down to allow healthier, more life-giving trees to be planted and nurtured? What had been planted before us by our ancestors was not our fault, but dealing with what remained now was our responsibility.

I often heard my friends of color call on the strength of those who came before them. They had a clear desire to be good ancestors, to leave the world better for the ones to come. I was envious of their connection to their families both past and future. My friend bought her son a shirt with "I am my ancestors' greatest dream" written across the front. It was powerful to watch this little Black boy run around the halls of preschool wearing it.

Was I my ancestors' greatest dream? I honestly wasn't sure.

I spent time staring out at my own family field, looking for clues.

Several years ago, old letters and family photographs were found in my great-aunt's attic. My mom's cousin did the incredibly time-consuming work of organizing them by date and having them typed out and bound with old photographs in a beautiful blue leather book. When I received it, I placed it on the bookshelf in our living room, where it mostly stayed put. (I realize the privilege of my actions—I could choose when to look at the history handed to me by simply opening a book. How many people would give almost anything to know more about their families' origins and history?) Until the day I was cleaning off the shelf.

As I glanced through it, I came upon a photograph of my great-grandfather graduating from Oberlin Theological Seminary in Ohio. Next to the picture was the text of a sermon he preached in 1910.

> But how is brotherhood to solve the race problem? Simply by instilling in the mind of the Native American, the immigrant, the Negro, the idea of common relationships, common duty, and a common destiny. Let the newcomer and the black man know that what is meant by the American spirit is a most perfect and cordial understanding between men . . . that in America men strive to be brothers. . . . It remains for you and me, his next door neighbors, to treat him in such a manner that he may know that he has friends

and a country. Then we shall behold a new America in which there is no longer any race problem.

The directness of the sermon pulled me in. Its obvious comfort with the subject matter of race and immigration surprised me. I read these words quickly and hungrily, trying to make sense of them.

No one would call this a Black liberation theology sermon. It was an incredibly idealistic and rather naive attempt at addressing hundreds of years of painful history and a current reality that needed a bit more than the golden rule to solve. And yet, at a time of resurgence for groups like the Ku Klux Klan, when there was a rising fear of the other, my ancestor preached acceptance and welcome.

It would be easy to assume that this story summed up my great-grandfather's views.

I continued to search the book for more insights when the words "Papa's Indian Story" leaped off the following page. *Who was "Papa"?* I wondered as I began to read, nervously. Likely an ancestor of mine. Likely someone who shared my family tree, my DNA, my name.

My heart started racing as I read it. I quickly figured out Papa was the same great-grandfather I had seen in the photograph, the same one whose sermon I had just read.

"Tell us a story, Papa. Tell us a story . . . about the Indians!"

"My father," began Papa, "came to this state a long time ago. There were very few White folks here then. He had Indians for his nearest neighbors. He soon learned their ways, and they seem to have liked him, for they never gave him any trouble."

The story took an unexpected turn when Papa's father thought it would be funny to administer a dangerous shock treatment "as a joke" to see if the "Indian" neighbor was lying about his back pain. I imagined my great-grandfather laughing as he read with his children, with my grandfather, all huddled in bed together, hooked on every word of this strange and cruel story. The page I read from concluded with, "Is that all? Is there any more to tell? Please, Papa, tell us another Indian story."

I closed the book, my face flushed as tears ran slowly down my cheeks. In some ways, I wasn't surprised to have found it because I had seen enough of White supremacy to know it could exist anywhere, even in a child's bedtime story. I wondered if my grandfather had repeated this story for my own mother when she was a child. When I asked her and my aunt later, neither had any memory of it.

My mind shifted between these two very different readings. Alone, they made sense. Together, they were such a deep and profound contradiction. In essence, my great-grandfather preached a sermon of brotherhood on Sunday morning, and then, as he tucked his children in at night, he told a bedtime story that mocked Indigenous neighbors.

I felt as if the story of Whiteness had just fallen in my lap—the twisted, subtle, overt, and contradictory story of Whiteness.

It would be tempting to say that just one side showed my "true" great-grandfather. That he was really an open-minded man who preached about and truly believed in the brotherhood of all races. Or that he was a deeply racist and prejudiced man, perpetuating and teaching White supremacy to his own children.

What was so unsettling was that there were elements of truth to both aspects.

This was in my blood. Literally. I didn't get to bleed out the racist parts of my family history that upset me. I didn't get to determine that my great-grandfather was either good or bad, only one thing or the other.

But this wasn't just about my great-grandfather. I myself was a jumble of stories marked by love and courage and standing up against racism, as well as times of silence, ignorance, and complicity. And this wasn't anything new. Was racism not also found in the story of America and the contradictions within Whiteness itself? For starters, our White founding fathers wrote and proclaimed, "We hold these truths to be self-evident, that all men are created equal," while viewing other men, women, and children as property and treating their own dogs and horses better than the human beings they felt entitled to enslave.

Often, the contradictions aren't obvious. Often, we defend someone we love, excusing away their racism or prejudice because we have seen them care for their family or defend their country, or simply because we believe them to be "good."

One night, a racial justice training I was coleading ended with an older White man yelling and asking who was *really* in charge (since in his mind it couldn't possibly be the Black woman leading the class). His wife came over to the high-top table I was standing at; as he attempted to walk off his anger, she explained that he was really a loving man who wanted to create jobs for the Black community and inspire Black kids on the South Side of Chicago and, and, and . . . "He really just wants to help," she concluded as they left the room together. I couldn't process what was more shocking—the man's actions or his wife's defense of them.

I looked out at my metaphorical field and found both kinds of trees taking up space. It was up to me to decide what I would pass down and what I would root out. But I couldn't do either without first honestly naming both—not to condemn, but to see the past more precisely and begin to move toward healing.

It is incredibly difficult, if not impossible, to heal what you don't name.

This is generational work. It will not happen overnight. But I am committed to changing and challenging what I can today so my kids have a chance to change and challenge what they can with a healthier racial healing legacy behind them. I am determined to forge ahead, not stuck defending or being ashamed of the past, but moving toward something better and passing down a healthier field.

Those two conflicting stories I read showed me something else: the importance of what is caught and what is taught in families.

When I became a mom, I started paying more attention to the often-uttered parenting phrase "caught, not taught." It implies that, at the end of the day, our actions and behaviors are a more effective teaching tool than instructional teaching ever would be. One could argue that what my grandfather taught was at odds with what was caught.

In pursuing racial justice as a family, the spoken teaching moments with kids are not enough; they must *catch* us pursuing racial justice.

I am concerned that we as parents tiptoe around our words and cross our fingers that our kids pick up what we are throwing down. That we're a little unsure of what to do exactly, so we try a pinch of this, a splash of that, and hope that it all comes together in the end.

But the flourishing of all people is too important to leave to chance. We must take every opportunity we possibly can to face racism, to name it, and to take the never-ending steps needed to heal and grow.

● ● ●

This is work that has no limits, which means it is impossible to go "too far." Instead, many of us likely restrain ourselves from examining our lives and choices as thoroughly as is needed to create real change.

We often expect more for our kids (and from them) than we do of ourselves.

We diversify our children's bookshelves when our own bookshelves are predominantly White, when our own marble jar is one color, or when we only read authors of color on subjects like racism or oppression.

We advocate for our children's school or church curriculum to be more representative or diverse while avoiding that email or meeting with our human resources team at work about hiring and retaining Black and Brown staff.

We encourage our children to be friends with any kids of color in their class, their team, or their youth group while our own small group, our friend circle, and our book club stay homogenous.

We teach our children that everyone is equal and that "sharing is caring" while using our time, voice, money, and votes to provide "the best [you name it]" for our own family at the potential expense of others. If my child's school is "the best," that means another child's is "the worst."

It starts with us, parents. We set the tone, the priority, the vision for our families. We decide what type of antiracism legacy we leave for our children to inherit. Our kids are watching. Are they confused? Or are we partnering with others to create a world that deals with the hard, the uncomfortable, the painful, the complex?

How will our kids know how to fix the problems of the world if they don't have a thorough understanding of what those problems are to begin with? Will they feel the weight on their shoulders alone because we've pushed it all on them? And will they take us seriously when we limit our involvement only to what we tell them to do, not what they catch us doing in our own lives and our own circles? Let's aim for caught *and* taught.

Justice is limitless and transformative. We cannot control it. Once we truly begin to pursue it, it will go wherever it likes—into every inch, pore, and crevice. Like rushing water, it is not concerned with rules but movement. So do yourself, your kids, and the world a favor: Don't try to contain justice, boxing it in to only where you are comfortable, passionate, knowledgeable, and confident. Don't try to keep your life safe, nonpolitical, unifying, and quiet. Don't let fear or old beliefs or family loyalty or people-pleasing hold you back.

Let justice run free. To free you. Me. Our kids. Each other. Us.

14

WIMPY WHITE BOYS

We don't really live in a culture that loves boys or loves children, and we don't encourage boys to be whole.

BELL HOOKS

It doesn't have to be this way.

ANDRE HENRY

MILO, OUR SECOND SON, WAS BORN ON A SATURDAY. His labor came on suddenly and unexpectedly, more than three weeks before his due date. Aside from an hour in the NICU for some breathing issues, he was doing well. I, however, was recovering from the shock of his arrival and the shock of what had happened earlier that same week.

The previous Tuesday was November 8, 2016—the date that Donald Trump won the United States presidential election. According to the Pew Research Center, 63 percent of White men voted for him. It was his second-largest single bloc of support, after nearly eight out of ten White evangelicals selected his name on the ballot. White women made up only slightly less of the Trump train than their male counterparts, and still, more voted for him than for his opponent, Hillary Clinton.

In some ways I was thankful my children were too young to ask me questions about why Trump talked so much about "building a wall" or what it meant to grab women or what his hand motions meant when he was impersonating a journalist with a disability. Although they couldn't ask these questions, I was pondering what a nation led by this man meant for the culture in which I was forced to raise my two White sons.

The name Milo means merciful and soft-hearted. It's also thought to be of Latin origin, meaning soldier. We chose it the morning he was born. "The world needs more mercy this week," my husband said as he held him in our hospital room. I loved the idea of those meanings dwelling deep inside him, because he would need to draw on both softness and strength as we prepared him to fight against so much.

So my interest was piqued when, a few hours after he was born, the nurse muttered over his cries, "Looks like we've got ourselves another wimpy White boy," as she took blood from a tiny hole poked in the bottom of his foot.

"What did you just say?" I replied, casually pulling up my robe as I spoke. Had she meant for me to hear? I gave her an encouraging look, and she went on.

"You mean 'wimpy White boy'?" She laughed. "It's nothing personal, it's just always the White boy babies that fuss the most in the hospital when I do the skin poke. They are often harder to calm down—more than any other boys of color and more than any of the girls. I'm not sure why exactly."

Her passing remark stayed with me. I learned that Wimpy White Boy Syndrome was actually a real term. According to one medical journal, it had to do with the survival rate of premature White males at birth compared to their peers. The conclusion of the article was that "the frailty of White males ends there."

Perhaps physically that was true. But was it just the beginning of a life marked by emotional and mental frailty?

Another shocking event had happened one week before Milo was born and three days before Trump was elected. As my family and I went for a walk in our neighborhood, I pushed Elliot in our beloved City Mini stroller with my father-in-law, stepmother-in-law, and John by my side.

It was a perfect fall day. I wore a light jacket, too tight to zip up over my swollen belly. We walked past the local brewery and our favorite little sandwich shop. As we passed the downtown train station, we heard the familiar bells and saw the railroad crossing posts go down into position as the red warning lights flashed. I spun Elliot's stroller around so we could all watch the train.

At that moment, someone ran from a nearby bench toward the train tracks.

"He's not going to make the train," we all said to each other. Then, time seemed to slow down. The blood drained from my face. I felt cold. Everything went quiet except for the sound of the train's horn, louder and longer with each passing second. The brakes screeched, but it was too late.

As quickly as I turned Elliot to see, I spun him back around, trying to block his view.

The train passed and came to a stop, just a few hundred feet from the station. We looked to the other side of the street where we hoped this young man, confused about which side the train was arriving, would be standing—the story I was telling myself. My father-in-law was the first to say, "He didn't make it."

As John called 911 and reported what had happened, I stayed further back with Elliot, still safe in his stroller. Still blocked from what had just occurred.

I listened to John describe what he had witnessed and watched him walk closer to the body to try to describe his age and physical characteristics (young White male) to the emergency operator. He came back with tears in his eyes, and we all just hugged as we waited for the paramedics to arrive. When they did, it only took a few minutes before they simply placed a sheet over the body. There was nothing they could do.

We watched the train conductor come over and talk to the paramedics. He was clearly distraught.

And then, not sure what else to do, we continued on our walk. I kept refreshing my phone and waiting for the internet to give me some news, hoping the incident would be covered and needing to know if he did it on purpose. I kept thinking of the boy's mother, how strange it was that I knew of her son's death before she did.

The next morning, I clicked on the headline "Man fatally struck by Metra train" and saw his name, that he was twenty-six years old, and that the coroner's office had ruled it a suicide.

I wept.

I don't pretend to know anything about this person's life, nor am I saying that struggling with mental health issues in any way makes one weak. But when that nurse called out Milo as a wimpy White boy, I didn't just think about Milo, or about a man just voted into office who proudly spoke of grabbing and kissing women, who called Mexican immigrants rapists and criminals, and whose business had been sued for racial discrimination as far back as the 1970s. I also thought about that young White man not making it across the tracks.

What leads White men to account for nearly 70 percent of suicide deaths? Why have White men committed more mass shootings than any other group? Why is accessing violence and anger seemingly so natural for them? And do we have any chance at challenging this weakness and frailty spun as strength and masculinity?

I searched outside of my own musings and found the writings of author, professor, and social activist bell hooks to be especially illuminating, shedding some much-needed understanding on these questions for me (and creating some new questions to consider as well). In her book *The Will to Change: Men, Masculinity and Love*, she ponders the pain of being a man in our society:

> These men suffer. Their anguish and despair has no limits or boundaries. They suffer in a society that does not want men to change. . . . Rather than acknowledge the intensity of their suffering, they dissimulate. They pretend. *They act as though they have power and privilege when they feel powerless. Inability to acknowledge the depths of male pain makes it difficult for males to challenge and change patriarchal masculinity* (emphasis mine).

According to a 2014 study, White men are 31 percent of the US population but hold 65 percent of all elected offices. White men have eight times as much political power as women of color. Almost 90 percent of the Fortune 500 CEOs are still White males. What is causing these feelings of powerlessness? Do the White men who are not in positions of such power and prestige believe that if they keep playing by the rules of White male supremacy, they too can end up at the top? Do the White men already in these positions of power have a deep fear that they will lose a White male supremacy that has been well-maintained for generations? I heard once that we maintain things that will eventually die. Are those at the top scared that their power will die on their watch, knowing or believing that they don't have the skills to survive without dominance and violence and control?

I thought back to something else I had learned from bell hooks: in healthy cultures, "males do not have to prove their value and worth. They know from birth that simply being gives them value, the right to be cherished and loved." But in our culture, "we don't encourage boys to be whole." So, men rely on their ability to dominate in order to believe themselves worthy of love.

We live in a society that shouts to men, "Put all your eggs in the power and domination basket, and ignore how you will have nothing left over for the other baskets"—the love, vulnerability, creativity, resilience, empathy, connection, and "I am loved for who I am" baskets. So, while White men might be dominating in some very real ways, they are unpracticed and weak practically everywhere else. They are not encouraged or expected to be whole human beings.

Hugh Mackay is an Australian social researcher and novelist who studies social trends. According to Mackay, "The experience of wholeness equips us to enter into the distress, the disappointment, the suffering of others, to bask with those who want us to share their fleeting moments of triumph, and to be reliably present for those grappling with life's uncertainties."

When you haven't faced challenges because of your gender or skin color, when the whole world has been set up by people who look like you to make life easier for you, and when you are the center of the center, you are less practiced at dealing with disappointment and disadvantages, hardship and pain. This is not to say you don't have problems—they just aren't likely rooted in your being male and White. You didn't lose out on a job interview solely because your name sounded Black, you didn't need a petition or bill created for you to be able to wear your hair the way it grows out of your head, you didn't have to prep your partner to advocate for you while in labor because as a Black woman your pain is often dismissed, and you weren't late to work thirty times because your job was in a nearly all-White, upper-class neighborhood and you were pulled over by the police for no reason other than driving as a Black man, like one colleague I know.

When you aren't given tools like vulnerability and empathy and emotions beyond anger and rage because of your maleness, what starts out as wimpy when you are young can easily become toxic and more dangerous as you grow older. It is easier to dehumanize others when you haven't connected with the fullness of your own humanity.

● ● ●

A year after Milo was born, our family of four attended a minor league hockey game. My husband was raised in Minnesota, where hockey is a way of life, but I was still somewhat new to the sport. I wore Milo in a carrier, and we ate nachos and warm pretzels covered in so much salt I had to dust it onto the floor before passing it to Elliot. It was really fun until a fight broke out between two players on the ice. This was not my first hockey game, and I understood that fights broke out all the time. It was, however, my first hockey game with my young boys, and I was seeing it through their eyes, especially three-year-old Elliot's.

People who had been talking to each other before were now glued to the center of the ice, where multiple players were throwing punches and shoving each other. Then the crowd erupted. "Fight! Fight! Fight!"

chanted three men two rows behind us. "Fight! Fight! Fight!" shouted the Boy Scout troop the next section over. "Fight! Fight! Fight!" the arena demanded.

As Elliot began to look around, wide-eyed at the commotion, I screamed over the crowd, "Elliot, look at Daddy!" I didn't know what to do to get the crowd to stop, but I could at least attempt to distract him until it calmed down. John understood my cry for help and started talking to Elliot about the game, but my preschooler did not understand. He kept asking why he needed to look away. I couldn't explain to him that he was being introduced to a part of toxic masculinity I loathed: the titillation of violence.

The next day on the way to lunch, I told my friend, a coworker who worked with junior high students, about the game. "We spend so much time telling our kids things like, 'Hands are for helping, not for hurting.' It felt so strange to watch people chanting the opposite message in front of them. I was not prepared for a moment like that. And before you tell me, please know that I am very aware that they can't be shielded forever. But I didn't know what else to do."

"Jenny," she began, "what do you know about salmon?"

I laughed, surprised, but trusting she was about to make a point, I confessed that the only thing I knew about salmon was that they are delicious.

"True," she agreed with a smile. As we walked, she explained that salmon endure an incredibly difficult and extremely demanding journey to swim upstream, where they will reproduce. "Like the salmon, you have to be strong enough to swim upstream, to challenge the culture we're all swimming in. And then you have to trust that your boys will be strong enough to follow your lead and keep going, even when you aren't around to show them the way."

I thought back to the moving sidewalk example I had first heard about in our trainings when we were defining racism. I realized that the overwhelming thought of the future my boys were facing was causing me to spiral. But the salmon analogy made sense, and I thanked my friend.

"It's how we coach junior high parents," she continued. "They often need to be reminded that their job isn't to remove their kids from the parts of culture that feel unsafe or that misalign with their values, but instead to equip their kids to know how to handle things when they come their way."

There was nothing I could do to protect my boys from the allure of Whiteness, the invitation to the patriarchy party. But I could make sure they saw it clearly and were offered lots of opportunities to go against the flow of the isms plaguing the cultural current.

● ● ●

Dr. David G. Oelberg has yet to meet a parent who has "expressed offense or disgust" at the term *wimpy White boy*. In fact, "most White parents find the term somewhat endearing because it highlights their roles in the ongoing provision of extra nurturing and patience."

It is our instinct to want to nurture our kids. In many ways, it's a no-brainer to want them to suffer less. But what if it tips past the point of being the best thing for them? In Romans 5:3-4, Paul wrote, "Suffering produces endurance, and endurance produces character, and character produces hope." If we trust that passage, which sounds like another vote in favor of wholeness, suffering should not be seen as the worst outcome. Instead, kids without endurance, character, and hope should be of greater concern.

And is our concern really grounded in them suffering less or in them fulfilling an expectation about what it means to be a man?

We tell boys they can belong as long as they fit in and then show them a box that can barely hold anyone. When we say "act like a man" or "man up," we expect a performance around gender. American gender theorist and philosopher Judith Butler explains: "When we say gender is performed, we usually mean that we've taken on a role or we're acting in some way and that our acting or our role playing is crucial to the gender that we are and the gender that we present to the world." We hand our boys a script and costumes and say, "Read this and wear these clothes like you are in a play and they will protect you." Then we watch, surprised, when they memorize those lines, internalize them, shame and exclude anyone who goes off script, and hide or shut away their own desires. As a result, they never get to be their truest selves and become envious of anyone who can.

The script they are being handed is a death sentence—for everyone. Going off script is swimming upstream. Going off script requires resistance. Going off script allows space for our wimpy White boys to challenge and resist what others do not. It gives them a chance to have a whole and beloved life as wholehearted White boys. Acting no longer required.

15

"MOMMY, WHO IS GEORGE FLOYD?"

*They believe that no one in their community is racist and
the best evidence for this is that nobody talks about race.*

MARGARET A. HAGEMAN

It is easier to build strong children than to repair broken men.

FREDERICK DOUGLASS

"Mommy, what's coronavirus?"

"Mommy, when will we get to go back to school?"

"Mommy, will it be like this forever?"

I was being asked so many new questions and had grown comfortable admitting I had no answers.

And then there were questions I had answers to that I needed to decide how to share.

One afternoon Elliot was taking a bath, his five-year-old body so long and lanky he nearly filled up the entire tub, leaving little room for his foam letters and tugboats and squishy penguins that shot out water through their mouths. I was trying to figure out how to tell him about what was happening in Minnesota as millions around the world watched the video of George Floyd's murder. It was recorded only a few miles from where his dad grew up and just a few more miles away from where two of his grandparents lived now.

We had been visiting the Twin Cities the last time all the eyes of the world focused on the Midwest, when thirty-two-year-old St. Paul Public School worker Philando Castile was murdered in front of his family. Elliot was just shy of two years old when that happened. John and I had walked around one of Minnesota's many lakes, trying to wrap our heads around another loss of life, another story that kept getting replayed. Elliot had been too young then to even understand what we were saying.

But he wasn't today.

Earlier in the week I had talked to a friend, a former first-grade teacher who encouraged me to present the situation to Elliot as calmly as I could. My husband and I planned to talk to him together later that day. *After* his bath.

I was sitting next to the tub, scrolling through my phone as it filled up with posts from protests in Minnesota, Chicago, Los Angeles, and New York. I was deeply moved by footage from a protest that observed eight minutes and forty-six seconds of silence—the amount of time the officer's knee was on George Floyd's neck, slowly and painfully, cruelly and casually snuffing out his light and life. I was so drawn in by the moment I almost forgot that Elliot sat less than two feet from me.

"Mommy, what's that noise?"

"It's a siren from this video of a protest I'm watching. Do you know what a protest is?"

Elliot shook his head, a few beads of water falling down the back of his neck.

"It's when a group of people come together to say they are upset about something and are trying to make things fair and equal."

I showed him my phone screen, thankful to have stumbled into a calm way of introducing something so alarming. We watched together for a few moments as the video panned across the crowd of people who were mostly sitting or on their knees. When the silence ended, a

Black man spoke loudly into a megaphone, his voice magnified into the crowd.

"George Floyd!" the crowd chanted.

"Mom, now what are they saying?"

"They're saying a man's name—George Floyd."

"Who's George Floyd? And why are they shouting his name?"

I'm not sure how much time went by while I considered how to answer. Enough time to remember that I had recently learned Floyd was a father. His daughter was just six years old, practically the same age as my son, who was waiting for me to hand him something that would help him make sense of what he was seeing and hearing. Enough time for me to think that if Floyd's daughter didn't get to be protected from the pain of racism, then neither did my son by learning about it.

I took a deep breath. "He was a Black man who lived in Minnesota, and people are sad because he was killed by a White police officer over the officer's feelings about the color of George Floyd's skin."

Elliot's face changed when my voice shook over the word *killed*. He blinked rapidly, trying to make sense of what I had just said, as some of his innocence evaporated into thin air. He looked to be in shock. I didn't know what I was expecting. We had been honest with him earlier that year that Martin Luther King Jr. had been killed because of racism and the work he was doing, so this wasn't a brand-new concept to him.

"But the police are supposed to help us." He spoke carefully but quickly, almost pleading with me to keep that idea intact.

How many myths do I address in one day? I wondered. The myth that every police officer really does protect and serve every person? The myth that there are only "good guys" and "bad guys"? The myth that everyone in the country was upset with this police officer's actions? The myth that this was the last time a Black man's name would be chanted at a protest?

"You're right, they are supposed to help. But this one didn't, so people are sad. And all over the United States they are trying to make things better."

"Are the police trying to make things better?"

"Some of them are. We can keep talking about this, okay? And you can let me or Dad know if you have any questions."

"I want to be out with those people."

"We will soon, babe."

Just as I started to relax, he added, "I'm glad I have White skin so I won't get shooted at."

And there it was. The underlying reason we were having this conversation, the reason why so many White people think they can stay out of the work: "I'm glad I have White skin so I won't (fill in the blank: be racially profiled, be wrongfully convicted, etc.)." We want our privileges to stay unexposed so we don't feel like hypocrites—so we don't have to acknowledge that we are neglecting the golden rule of treating others as we want to be treated.

We don't want to mess things up in case it disturbs our convenience. We prefer the comfort of the lie over the freedom of the truth. And since we're not the one shooting, we think we're forever innocent.

"Honey, no. Everyone should be safe around the police no matter who they are. We don't want to be safe while others have reason to be afraid. That's what we are working for, okay?"

"Okay," he replied as I finished bathing him, his pale White skin blending in with our beige tub. I tried to wash away the dirt and sweat and remnants of peanut butter and jelly. I tried to wash away the distancing and rationalizing I witnessed in his little mind.

A few days later, our family walked to our town's Black Lives Matter protest. We held signs that said "Families for Black Lives Matter" and, quoting Andre Henry, "It doesn't have to be this way." When the crowd shouted George Floyd's name, Elliot shouted "George Floyd" and "Black Lives Matter" right along with them—knowing the weight and truth of his words as much as a five-year-old can.

I share that bath story not to shame my young child but to point out that his supposed innocence toward race was simply not there to begin with. As early as six to nine months, babies start observing racial differences, and by three to five years old, White preschoolers exclude others based on race. White innocence is a myth at every age. Our children are not colorblind. And yet many White parents believe they shouldn't talk to their kids about racism because it's their job to not "rob them of a childhood" or "take away their innocence." But we are protecting them only from an illusion of a life devoid of racism and privilege. This denial ultimately protects White supremacy. Our role as White parents is to not keep the illusion of their innocence intact—especially not when this protection interferes with so much.

While the kids watched TV, I told John I had just talked to Elliot about George Floyd. I could tell he was disappointed not to have been there to help shape how our son was seeing the world and his place in it. But John and I were both well aware that this was the beginning of a dialogue. The ideas we talked about didn't just go down the drain with the bathwater. As parents, we must be committed not only to "the talk" but also to an ongoing conversation filled with questions we answer the best we can as they come, creating a space where our kids are conscious of and curious about color and its significance in their world.

One of the reasons we must be so committed to engaging our kids in conversations about racism is that so many others are not. There are very real forces at work keeping these conversations out of the norm. In fact, a survey conducted by *Sesame Street* found that just 10 percent of parents report they "often" talk to their kids about race, while 28 percent report they "sometimes" do. That's not even talking about how to be an antiracist—that's just talking about it *at all*. The chance my kids learn about race at other families' dinner tables or at school is highly unlikely. This work must be done by us. We are the best chance at disrupting racist ideas and dangerous ideologies.

Whenever I feel nervous or scared about getting it wrong, I remind myself of this simple truth: the only "wrong" way to do this is to not do it at all. To think that it is optional. To believe that our kids are automatically antiracist. Instead, we must recognize that racism is a moving walkway. And it's up to us to prepare our children to run in the opposite direction. But how does that look?

Many families use different approaches to talk about racism with their young children of color. Parents want their kids to enjoy a childhood with as much joy as possible. Several friends of mine did not discuss in depth the murders of George Floyd or Breonna Taylor with their young Black children, recognizing that the years of innocence around racism are so few. For one of my friends, it was already a lot to prepare her five-year-old daughter for the racism she might experience now, without also worrying about a family member experiencing a similar fate as Floyd one day. While race itself is discussed and celebrated in their home, they are choosing to hold off on some of the harder and heartbreakingly inevitable conversations with their kids.

This is not a one-size-fits-all family experience. And it's important to keep in mind that children will develop racial attitudes with or without our guidance as we parent within a racialized society. John and I are opting for *with* our guidance. Here are some of the approaches we are establishing for our family.

Recognize it's never too early. We can practice talking to our babies as soon as they are born. Will they understand anything we're saying? Nope. Will they remember it? Not a chance. But the purpose of this time is to get comfortable talking it through and working out any gaps so that when they do start absorbing what we say, we are familiar with talking to our child about race and racism. Normalize it early and often.

Many parents worry that introducing these ideas too early will lead their kids to notice race and racism "too much." That makes sense only if you think kids aren't already putting labels on everything, including humans, to make more sense of the world. But talking about these things early on allows you to be known as a resource and companion for the journey.

Start with diversity. Begin with celebration. Isn't it so cool that, for all we have in common, we are still so different? Different sizes, different genders, different skills and interests and ideas, different body and eye and nose shapes, different hair color and texture, and different skin colors. Learn about different cultures through food, museums, neighborhoods, music. Put language to the differences. Make the connection that, without difference, we wouldn't have clues as to who others are. These clues help us see each other. They are good—objectively good. After all, it's racism and other isms that are wrong, not the differences themselves.

I love how writer and civil rights activist Audre Lorde wrote about our differences: "When we define ourselves, when I define myself, the place in which I am like you and the place in which I am not like you, I'm not excluding you from joining—I'm broadening the joining."

Provide helpful and clear language. Our job is not to make our children feel better about the world. It's to invite, foster, and encourage them to be ready to deal with a complicated future. We don't get brave kids by keeping things from them or softening the lens through which they see. We must offer clear words and meanings that help them to grasp the world as it is and to better communicate what they would like it to be. As Brené Brown reminds us, "Clear is kind. Unclear is unkind. . . . Feeding people half-truths . . . to make them feel better (which is almost always about making ourselves feel more comfortable) is unkind."

In our family, we've found it helpful to start with a few kid-friendly definitions; they will need to evolve and deepen as our kids age, but having a shared language is crucial to ongoing conversation. The key is to start small and keep building. Use these definitions to address things that have happened throughout history and that are ongoing today.

"Racism is all the ways the world works to be easier and better for people who have White skin like us, and harder for people who don't." I borrowed this definition from my friend Meredith. It's helpful because it points to systems and structures; the language "White skin like us" identifies places of privilege that we (White parents and families) are included in, instead of letting us distance ourselves from White people and making it seem like we're the "good ones."

A fantastic way to talk to our kids about White privilege centers around the idea of "fair" and "unfair," which is likely part of their language already. It allows us to build on the racism definition: "White privileges are the ways the world makes it easier for White people to get

more—more money, more advantages, more power, more education—
than anybody else. This is unfair, and it also means White people are
treated better: they are disciplined less harshly in school, they're stopped
less by the police, and even things like Band-Aids often come in a color
that matches their skin."

"Prejudice is when someone isn't just mean to someone else
because they don't like them; they're mean because of something
related to that person's identity, like their skin color or the kind of
church they go to. Can you think of someone we've learned about
who experienced prejudice?"

"A microaggression is a sneaky way of being racist. Even though it can
seem nice, it's really hurtful to the person hearing it. An example would
be, 'You're really pretty for a Black girl' or, 'I thought all Asians were good
at math.' Why do you think either of those would be racist to say?"

Prevent unlearning. Maybe this goes against what you have heard
before—that an important component in our antiracism journey is to
unlearn racist, Whitewashed history and relearn the truth. While this is
certainly key, I'm saying that if our kids learn the truth of our country's
origins first, they won't need to spend time and energy in the future
unlearning lies; they'll have a jump-start to their own antiracism journey. I want my kids to not be at the same starting line I began at so they
can go even farther than I will.

Ask your child's teacher at the beginning of the year if and how topics
like multiculturalism—including but not limited to Hispanic Heritage
Month, Black History Month, and Asian American and Pacific Islander
Heritage Month—will be taught and represented visually in the classroom. Email the administration and ask directly what their antiracism
plan is. Be prepared to share resources and research. Inquire into how
world history will be taught. Who are the "heroes" and "sheroes" of history according to their textbooks and lessons?

Change their experiences. Our kids construct meaning from experience, so as we shift our actions and behaviors from neutral to antiracist,
their brains will reconstruct to make sense of the new experiences.

Bring your kids to marches and protests. Create traditions around visiting museums on Martin Luther King Jr. Day, or exploring your city's Chinatown during AAPI Heritage Month, or volunteering with a food pantry or refugee resettlement agency. Have your kids write letters to their local representative. Take them on a field trip to your state capitol and arrange a meeting with someone who works on policies your family cares about. Host a fundraiser and let them do research and pick where the donation goes. Encourage them to see the problems and the solutions. Invite them to dream and imagine the world being more just. Provide on-ramps for ownership in their pursuit of antiracism.

No one grows when they're comfortable. Do things that make you and your kids uncomfortable, and you will be on the path toward growth.

Have a compelling "why." Before you get bogged down by the question "What are we going to do about racial injustices?" be honest about your family's reason for engaging in the first place. What is your why? Are you doing this because you think it's the right thing to do? Because it's a reflection of your faith or values? Are you trying to create a better world for yourself and those around you? My friend shared that her family is doing the work not so her kids will have the virtue of being antiracist but so their friends will lead lives in which they are honored, dignified, and able to flourish. Create the why together. Push yourself and your family past a reason steeped in guilt or shame that won't sustain you or inspire you to keep at it.

No shushes and no shame. If you've ever played the game "Eye Spy" with a child, you know how important color is to them. It's usually our first method as parents to help our kids explain the world. My kids learned colors before numbers and their ABCs. So if something as foundational as color appears off-limits only when it comes to the subject of skin color, that will be a clear outlier from all the other ways you use it to describe the world.

When Elliot was three, we started teaching him about Martin Luther King Jr., focusing a lot more on his life than how he died in order to be age-appropriate. We were in the courtyard outside his preschool when, in the distance, we saw the father of one of his classmates. Usually the child's White mother dropped him off, but today it was his dad, a Black man in his early thirties. As we walked a little closer Elliot started getting physically excited. "Is that Martin Luther King Jr.?" he asked with great enthusiasm.

"No, bud. Remember, Martin Luther King Jr. is no longer alive. So that can't be him, right? I think that's Henry's dad."

"Oh, right," he laughed as he realized his mistake.

"But they do both have a similar skin color—how would you describe it?" I asked, wanting to continue the conversation.

"Maybe like chocolate milk?"

"Oh, yeah, I totally see that too. I love chocolate milk! And I think that's how they describe someone's skin color in the book we read the other night, right?"

"Oh, yeah!"

I don't know what I would have done had I not been prepared for that moment. I could have easily told him to lower his voice or that we would talk about it later, or even offered a judgment on his observation. Instead, I resisted any feelings of embarrassment or shame because I wanted to be clear that his questions, observations, and mistakes were all better than silence. I tried to keep in mind the larger message Elliot would take away. At the end of the day, I am committed to enduring a bit of embarrassment or discomfort so long as it continues the questions, the curiosity, the challenging, the learning, and ultimately, the dismantling of harmful and deadly constructs for my child. It's an opportunity to swim upstream against the social politeness that keeps parents more upset about their child being perceived as rude than about the violence and oppression that feed off our silence. (In this instance, the father was far out of earshot—but if he had heard, I would have checked in with him and offered something like, "I don't know if you heard my son's question about you, but if you did and were bothered by it, I'm sorry.")

I want to hear my kids' questions and what they are processing, because those are clues to how they make sense of the world. I don't want to lecture them; I want an ongoing dialogue. I want anything that creates more learning, more growth, more progress. And I want to learn with them.

Some things we have been taught are not effective at challenging racism. The following is a (non-exhaustive) list of things that don't work.

Colorblindness. Pretending there is no significance to the racial caste system.

Stopping at diversity. Celebrating diversity and then pushing the message that "we're all equal" is not the goal either—in fact, it's insufficient. Our differences are not equal. So while acknowledging our differences is an important step, it's not enough to address racism. As author Jennifer Harvey writes in her book *Raising White Kids,*

> If we lived in a diverse society that was equal and fair in terms of racial treatment, valuing difference would be sufficient. Saying we're all 'just different, let's celebrate' would be great. But we live in a society in which White people receive benefits, protections, and privilege in systemic ways, while children of color do not.

Celebrating diversity should lead to a better understanding of inequality—for example, as a family we can talk about discrimination in our immigration system and brainstorm ways to raise money and use our voices to stand with families broken apart at the US-Mexican border due to an unjust system.

Racism aging out of existence. It might be tempting to look at this country's history of forced legal segregation and think, "There is so much more diversity in schools than when I was a kid. *It's so much better today.*" To that I would ask, "On whose terms is it better?" Just because it's objectively better than chattel slavery and Jim Crow laws and Japanese internment camps doesn't mean that it's completely right or just or equal or fair. Or that there is no more work to be done that could create a world of flourishing for all people.

One of the advantages to Elliot being home for school during parts of the Covid-19 pandemic was that I got to hear how his first-grade teacher handled topics like Martin Luther King Jr. Day. I stood outside his bedroom door and listened to her talk about this brave man who stood for equality and fair treatment. I held my breath as she read a book on Rosa Parks and then explained that, unfortunately, there was still so much to do to continue Martin and Rosa's work. It was such a simple but vital thing to add. She did not tie up history with a nice neat bow, as we are often tempted to do. She left it messy and in the present.

● ● ●

How do we know if what we're doing is working? What are we having these conversations and experiences and doing this ongoing work for—to solve or fix racism? Yes, although that's not likely to happen without significant structural change. To lessen harm and decrease interpersonal racism, and increase awareness and be open to transformation? That is a more realistic goal and involves the following.

A meaningful dialogue on race and racism. A dialogue that is open-ended, ongoing, and discussed by both kids and grownups. It involves asking lots of questions and poking at how and why the world works, all through a racial lens.

Antiracist attitudes and beliefs. A growing understanding of White privilege as an injustice and something unfair, not something that is deserved or a "blessing."

Racial self-awareness and a commitment to challenging racism whenever we encounter it. Children of color experience pride in the representation of their culture and heritage, and White children are empowered knowing they can be part of the solution.

● ● ●

No matter what, it's *never* too late. So you didn't start talking to your six-month-old about the beauty of different skin tones and hair types. So you did all the things that don't work and none of the things that do. So your kids know no one of color or anyone different from you or your family. So what! You start where you are, not where you wish you were. There is no better day to begin than today. And be encouraged—just one week of intentional and meaningful conversations on race can change a child's perception.

Our antiracism growth should become part of the framework of our parenting. When we talk about bullying, incorporate antiracism. When we talk about problem solving, incorporate antiracism. When we teach our kids to be generous and share, incorporate antiracism. We don't have to force these concepts because they already intersect with what we talk to our kids about daily. We must take risks by parenting in an intentional, imaginative way that might not be based on what our neighbors are doing or what our own parents did with us. It's not easy, but it is critical.

Do literally whatever you must to bring up topics of race and antiracism. It doesn't have to be a nightly after-school special (I hope that isn't such a dated reference that you don't know what I'm talking about), just a part of your regular conversations. It's okay if it feels forced at first. It's like anything new—it will take time. The important thing is to be intentional and consistent. You can tell your children you are learning, too. Modeling learning and vulnerability has the power to raise a generation with the tools to tackle the mess of racism.

Because it *is* a mess, y'all. And addressing a mess is often messy. If you've ever reorganized any part of your home, you know this to be true. You stand before your closet/pantry/dresser and think, *How much stuff could I possibly have?* When you take everything out (if you're like me), you are overwhelmed at the mess. You don't know what to do. You regret taking it on in the first place. You now have three choices: (1) Shove everything back in and deal with it later; (2) take the time to meet the mess, examine each item, decide what stays and what goes, come up with a system so it doesn't get so messy so easily; or (3) leave it for someone else to clean up.

If my generation opts for the third choice, we are leaving it to our kids to clean up. On their behalf, I'm resentful. I'm imagining them coming home from school and finding a mess they didn't make without any guidance on how to tackle it. That sucks. Let's deal with the mess, even if it means we're overwhelmed. Even if it means it takes time and we have to maintain it every day. Let's make it right for everyone, at long last.

Now That We're Clearer on the What,
Let's Talk About the When

We don't start our toddlers on calculus or *Moby Dick*. We start with one, two, three, and ABC. We break it down into age-appropriate blocks, knowing we can't skip over the foundations if we ever want our children to grasp these concepts. The same is true for raising antiracist kids. We don't have a one-and-done talk that addresses everything or reactive conversations based on what they're hearing from their friends. Instead, we have a thousand little conversations throughout their childhood, we introduce frameworks and understanding consistently and over time. We create an environment in which ideas and concepts build on each other. Here are some of your building blocks:

Ages 0–3

Make differences normal! Show your kids diversity through everything— the toys they play with, the books they read, the shows they watch. Practice talking about color. Use different colors in your drawings of people.

Ages 4–5 (Preschool)

These are the concrete thinking ages. Kids start wanting to know the "why" and the "how" of everything. Lean into that. Teach them the basics of why we have different skin colors to begin with (the answer is melanin). They also want to categorize everything, so you can help give appropriate and accurate labels. At this age, they move beyond "I have peach skin and she has chocolate skin" to "I have skin we call White and she has skin we call Black." Real-life situations allow us to engage beyond theory—ask them what they think of their own questions to help guide your answers.

When Elliot was in preschool, a White boy in his class told the only Black girl that she and another White boy couldn't get married because of the color of their skin. The teacher shut it down quickly and explained that it wasn't true. When I asked Elliot that night if people with different colored skin could get married, and he replied, "I think so, but why would that boy say that," we were able to have a simple conversation (he was four after all) about history and the way rules (a.k.a. laws) can change to be more fair.

But without a very direct talk, he likely would have sat with that question for much longer.

Grades K–3 (Early Elementary)

These are the ages we go beyond the concepts of diversity and representation and start introducing a deeper understanding of racism, including the general history of Indigenous land, slavery and abolition, Jim Crow, Japanese internment camps, and the civil rights movement. Kids of all colors learn about people throughout history who challenged racism, which helps to enforce the reality that we are joining with others in history who came before us. Continue to reject the belief that this knowledge will somehow destroy their innocence. Engage in conversations about differences and poke holes in stereotypes they see both in real life and in the media. Establish yourself at your child's school as a family committed to antiracism.

Grades 4–6 (Upper Elementary)

At this age, kids will have more in-depth history lessons on topics such as lynching, how neighborhoods were created through redlining, and why there is such a large wealth gap among races. These lessons point to the systems and structures that make up our society and challenge the hyper-individualized ways racism exists (i.e., racist people doing harm through personal interactions versus creating systems that perpetuate racism).

Introduce Dr. Beverly Tatum's moving walkway concept: "I sometimes visualize the ongoing cycle of racism as a moving walkway at the airport. Active racist behavior is equivalent to walking fast on the conveyor belt."

That is such a powerful and clear metaphor, and not just for our kids. It also helps us to visualize our role and the importance of taking action rather than avoiding what we might consider racist action. What steps can you encourage your kids to take to practice using their lives for change? I bet if you ask them, they have some ideas. Or, better yet, start by asking all kids, "What problem do you want to solve when you grow up—and how can you start today, because you don't need to wait until you're a grownup to make things better?" instead of "What do you want to be when you grow up?" You can help guide them in whatever problem they care about—they can write letters to their representatives, create art as resistance and raise awareness, or volunteer with a food bank. Water their seed of interest and watch it grow and bloom into something beautiful and, even more importantly, something sustainable and worth building on.

Grades 7–8 (Middle School)

At this age, my mom first told me that old saying, "No one is thinking about you right now as much as you." And it's true! Kids have so much to figure out as they transition into their older-kid and young adult years. They are going inward, leaning in and processing their racial identity more than ever before. But it's not just all about them. They are growing their ability to empathize—so encourage their empathy, especially in cross-racial friendships, as this is often the age when, according to author Rebekah Gienapp in her book *Raising Anti-Racist Kids*,

> White middle schoolers might notice a growing distance between them and friends of color. One thing that adults can teach White children is that they should believe their friends of color who say they're experiencing racism. This might sound obvious, but so often White people react to claims of racism with questions that pick apart the incident. What's needed instead is empathy and support. Learning this habit helps White children become better allies. It can also have the side effect of helping kids maintain cross racial friendships.

Create safe spaces to help them process the parts of their identity they might struggle with, as their identity is tied to those who have been/are oppressed and those who have been/are the oppressors. Help give language to these feelings of guilt or shame that might be showing up. Encourage their desire to make change in their world.

This is likely the start of the onslaught of social media influence. I was alarmed to learn about White nationalist and alt-right groups' online strategies to recruit young boys starting at the age of eleven. They often use jokes and memes to normalize bigotry and provide many of their followers a sense of inclusion and purpose. It helps their followers answer the question, "Where do I belong?"

"Extremist recruiters understand," says Gil Noam, an associate professor of psychology at Harvard Medical School, "that a child at this age is more likely to respond to the pull of community and a sense of purpose, even if they don't readily identify with a group's core message. Even with the Hitler Youth, what they really understood was the power of belonging."

These are the ages at which ideas of justice become incredibly important and easier to manipulate without accurate historical context. It is crucial to consistently bring up the question "Who does this perspective serve to protect and who does it harm?"

It is critical to foster their desire for belonging and importance in antiracist ways.

High School

Study any resistance movement and you will quickly find young people and students at the forefront. We must take high school students seriously as they recognize their anti-establishment outlook and as we encourage them to harness fresh energy and insight against racist systems.

Watch documentaries on history and antiracism with them and see if that opens more doors of communication.

Further unpack the spectrum of privilege (beyond race) and use college application season and job applications to talk more deeply about the realities of systemic racism. Fight supremacy that's disguised as serving or volunteering, which is often referred to as "White saviorism."

• • •

This is a quick overview. I highly recommend the books *Raising White Kids* by Jennifer Harvey, *Why Are All the Black Kids Sitting Together in the Cafeteria* by Dr. Beverly Tatum, and *Raising Anti-Racist Kids* by Rebekah Gienapp, along with the Be The Bridge workshop "Talking to Kids About Race," all of which informed some of these frameworks and explore these topics more deeply.

16

THE GRAYNESS
OF BLACK AND WHITE

*Racism . . . is a set of socioeconomic traps and cultural values that are
fired up every time we interact with the world. It is a thing you have to
keep scooping out of the boat of your life to keep from drowning in it. I
know it's hard work, but it's the price you pay for owning everything.*

SCOTT WOODS

"MOM, I LIKE THIS ONE!" Elliot danced around the Halloween costume aisle at Target, giddy with delight as he pointed at the section dis-
playing Black Panther costumes. He had not yet seen the movie, but he
knew who Black Panther was. I had a conflicting reaction—on one hand,
I loved that he had chosen the only Black superhero out of a lineup of
superhero costumes. On the other hand, I wondered if this was a form
of cultural appropriation. I knew certain things were clearly off-limits—
dressing up as Native Americans, Blackface, derogatory depictions of
any race. But this felt unclear. I texted John and showed him the costume,
asking, "What do we think about Elliot being Black Panther?" A few seconds later, he sent a thumbs up emoji. I felt unsure even as I put it in
my cart.

"Is it cool with you if Elliot dresses up as Black Panther?" I asked one
Black friend before we headed over to her neighborhood to
go trick-or-treating.

"Yes, of course!" she replied without hesitation. "I think it's great that he chose Black Panther."

We set out to trick-or-treat with her family, including her husband, who was also dressed like Black Panther. We took pictures of him and Elliot in costume, both standing in the "Wakanda Forever" pose, arms crossed over their chests. Their young Black son was dressed up as Superman.

A few weeks later, I asked another Black friend as we caught up one night on the phone. "Elliot dressed up as Black Panther for Halloween. Do you have any thoughts on that?"

"*I* have no problem with that," she said, "but I know some Black people who might." This wasn't all that surprising and was partially why I had asked. Black people are not a monolith.

More digging was required.

The internet (unsurprisingly) provided no resounding clarity. There were arguments from all sides—it was acceptable for White people to dress up as long as the person was imaginary or the culture they were dressing up as wasn't real. Sterling K. Brown, an actor in the movie, said he "can't wait to see little White kids dressing up as Black Panther." And then, in the next click, it was never permissible—some things were only for the people group the character represented. I came upon a *New York Times* article titled "The Many Meanings of Black Panther's Mask." The author, Kwame Opam, spoke directly to the differing opinions. "At best, the character's get-ups speak to the enthusiastic embrace of a black superhero. At worst, they could be perceived as an unwitting form of cultural appropriation, which has in recent years become a subject of freighted discourse."

So which one was it? What was the "right" thing to do here? How do we make decisions when we don't feel confident in our choices? This has sarcastically been referred to as a "White-22"—feeling, as a White person, damned if you do and damned if you don't. The feeling that, no matter what, someone will be upset or angry or calling you out as a racist or encouraging you to re-examine your choices. This is sometimes met with the temptation to throw your pale arms up in the air, saying in frustration and anger that "this feels impossible" and "we can never get it right," and then throwing your arms back down along with any commitment to engage in the work.

One of my friends is a White mom raising two young Black daughters with her husband, who is also White. One night over wine and cheese, she told me about the tension she felt around doing their hair.

There are some people in the Black community who say the best thing for my girls is that I know how to take care of their hair—to watch YouTube videos or go to the Black stylist and learn from them. Then there are others who say that me doing their hair is depriving them of a connection with a Black experience—going to the beauty shop and adding another mirror of relational representation to their lives. I see both sides and it's hard to know what the best thing to do even is. If I do it myself, I'm not exposing my girls to the Black community, but if I don't, I'm outsourcing my work to a Black woman yet again. It is honestly really confusing knowing what's best.

I felt her longing for clarity, for a "right" or "best" way to handle this. But the truth was, both her options had good and bad sides because both were connected to a larger reality that these two young girls were being raised outside their Black culture, and both were attempts to make up for this unchangeable fact. When more closely examined, both options were connected to loss and, ultimately, to pain.

Hundreds of superheroes exist. What was remarkable about Black Panther was not that he was Black but that he was the first popularized Black superhero. Up until very recently, every time Black children wanted to dress up as a superhero for Halloween, they essentially had no options that looked like them. What did it say that, with all the options my kids already had, they wanted the one that wasn't made with them in mind? Could this be a time to invite them to consider that not everything is meant to belong to them?

My kids had recently been learning about the "main character" in stories. We would lie in bed at night after watching a movie or reading

a book and talk about the characters. It was such a natural way to introduce the notion of Whiteness: when someone with White skin is always
the main character, gets the most attention, and is in the most scenes.
Our family had just watched *Frozen II,* so we talked about the main
characters, Anna and Elsa, both White. This movie had more diversity
than the first one, yet we knew only a few characters of color by name,
and while the story touched on themes like colonialism, it was still told
almost exclusively through the eyes of White characters.

The significance of Black Panther could very easily be connected to
the pervasiveness of Whiteness. Beneath the pride surrounding this
Black superhero is the reality of his exceptionality.

But my thoughts shifted away from asking what was best for my
White son and instead toward what was best for our friend's young Black
son who had gone as Superman. Was he excited that Elliot had picked a
Black superhero? Or did it take away from the specialness of finally having a superhero that reflected him and his dad?

This might seem like a lot of thought over a Halloween costume. I
understand that. But if we aren't willing to interrogate a kid's Halloween costume, will we even examine more significant choices in our
own lives?

My takeaway from all this time spent processing isn't if we did the
right or wrong thing. My takeaway is that I'm thankful for the time I took
to ask, poke, learn, and ultimately understand better. I learned more
about cultural appropriation. I learned more about the importance of
representation. My efforts weren't wasted because they helped me
develop a framework for the gray areas, a framework that asks:

- Where can I find more research or data so I'm not solely dependent
  on the people of color most impacted by this topic in my life to
  teach me?

- Who are the trusted people from the Black, Indigenous, Latinx, and
  AAPI communities (and knowledgeable White people) with whom
  I can process these complicated and nuanced ideas if I'm still con-
  fused after further research?

- How can I decenter myself in the process?

This framework has become my proverbial fishing rod—instead of constantly asking for more "fish," for more right answers from others, for more approvals or thumbs downs, I have tools to use for a lifetime.

As a parent, one thing frustrates me most about helping my kids with their schoolwork: their demand to "just tell me the answer!" Since they are young, sometimes I do offer the first answer as a freebie, as a chance for them to know it and have a new understanding click in their minds. But after that, they need to learn how to get to the answer on their own.

Parents need the same thing. After a while, our demands to "just tell me the answer" sound about as annoying and childish as when our kids approach learning the same way. And sometimes, the answer is simply, "It's complicated."

Friends, we are not children. We have gone to college and figured out careers and remodeled our homes and filed our taxes. We are smart and capable. We just have to be willing to learn. Our goal can't be to just avoid "looking racist" or "doing the wrong thing." We are operating with an uncompelling motive in which the only thing we aim for is less wrong. There is little room for imagination in that approach.

We act as if there are perfect rules to not being racist—airtight, nuance-free rules. There are some, for sure, such as the ones we've likely heard over and over: slavery was evil; Blackface isn't okay; White people can't say the N-word. But those are just the tip of the iceberg. We have to dive deeper and develop an ability to breathe in murky waters, or risk drowning.

There is no "just" in justice. "I'll just go to a Black church. I'll just send my kids to a more diverse school. I'll just get out to vote. I'll just support Black-owned businesses. I'll just get it all right." Our "just" puts limits on justice. I think we want rules because we believe this work can be done perfectly or we somehow can skate over it, mistake-free. "If we just know all the rules, we can win this game." The extremes of black and white, right and wrong provide comfort in the certainty that we are on the right side—of history, of the argument, of every line ever drawn.

White friends, we will never "win." We will continue to make mistakes. We will be silent when we should have said something. We will speak when we should have listened. We will say the wrong thing. We must let go of the illusion of doing this perfectly. Perfect allies are a myth, an illusory unicorn of White saviorism. "Perfect" has things under control—but control is the enemy of growth and liberation. We are in practice mode, always. Training mode, always. Learning and unlearning mode, always. Humility and teachability mode, always.

We will not arrive at antiracist status. No one is handing us a certificate of allyship. The principles we build in our children don't end with them. We must build them in ourselves so we can discern what is contributing to the gray. We must get better at sifting through the complexity of what racial justice looks like, based on our own digging into non-Whitewashed history and sociology and not just based off the one person of color we ask. We must not only discern the problems of our times but also work to understand how we got to those problems in the first place. Only then can we even attempt to come up with solutions.

We must remember that racism is in everything, all around us. It often manifests not as the obviously dangerous shark from *Jaws*, with the suspenseful score warning us of its impending arrival, but as the entire ocean itself.

And, many times, that means we must live in some gray. We must live in the tension. But we must not get stuck there. There is a lot to learn in the gray. The pursuit of perfection paralyzes movement, while the pursuit of progress energizes and empowers. We must chase after the "now that I know better, I do better" way of thinking that Maya Angelou set out for us. Aim for *better*, even if you have to fight your way through a lot of gray and uncertainty to keep going.

17

ON THE STREET WHERE YOU LIVE

*We are part of the society that we are fighting to change,
and we cannot absolve ourselves of our role in it.*

MIKKI KENDALL

*When we identify where our privilege intersects with somebody else's
oppression, we'll find our opportunities to make real change.*

IJEOMA OLUO

MY ORIGINAL INTENTION FOR THIS CHAPTER was to explore examples of abuse committed by men. I got the idea for this book when the #metoo and #churchtoo movements were becoming prominent. Everywhere I looked, from Hollywood to the Supreme Court, men—White men in particular—were being called to account for power abuse, assault, and harm. And that included the very church where I worked.

One night I found myself among thousands of people at church to hear what was going on after a well-circulated newspaper article had reported allegations against the senior pastor. For the next hour we heard a clear defense of his actions: the women involved were "liars" and "colluders" who were trying to destroy the senior pastor's "legacy."

The room offered him a standing ovation. It was nearly instantaneous and included almost everyone. Past the many legs now at my eye level, I glimpsed a few colleagues from my team who had also stayed seated. I was angry and confused. I knew some of the women he was name-calling, smearing, and dismissing.

The senior pastor was later further investigated, and the allegations of power abuse and sexual misconduct against him were found to be credible. He was forced to resign and was basically never heard from again. Where I had tiptoed in the organization in the past, I now felt permission to stomp. I leaned in, asked risky questions, and made my voice heard about power abuses, sexism, and racism I witnessed. I became brave in a new way.

And yet, something was still off. One afternoon, not long after that standing ovation occurred, I stormed into my coworker's office, fired up and frustrated.

"I'm sick of trying to make White men around me feel more comfortable," I practically yelled as I sat down. My White male coworker was seated at one end of the conference table, another White male colleague at the other end. I continued my rant. "Every time I say something about racism or sexism in the presence of White men, I find myself couching it with a defensive 'but I love White men—the three most important people in my life are my White husband and two White boys.' I am so sick of feeling like I will have a target on my back if I don't point my arrows away from the White men I'm around." Clearly, I felt very comfortable with these two particular White men. I was also fired up with a clear target in mind. It would feel so appropriate, so within bounds to spend this chapter going after that target, incident by incident, victim by victim, abuse by abuse. But why did I care about the comfort of White men at all? If explored, what would that ultimately reveal about me?

A friend told me once that the most dangerous people are often those who have been both the oppressed and the oppressor.

Jesus said, "You hypocrite, first take the plank out of your own eye, and then you will see clearly to remove the speck from your brother's eye" (Matthew 7:5 NIV). In wanting to explore examples of others' abuse, I realized I needed to take the plank out of my own eye first. The starting point for this conversation is a subject I'd rather avoid: myself and the group I most easily identify with, White women. Because of sexism and the patriarchy, we White women have absolutely experienced oppression. But because of racism and White supremacy, we have also perpetuated oppression. We are exactly who my friend was describing. We are not as sweet or nice as we would like to think; we as a whole are dangerous. In part because White women have been loyal to White men and to Whiteness for a long time without even realizing it. We have historically benefited more from our association with White men than any other group of people, including other women. And it has come at a cost.

As activist Rachel Cargle says in her lecture "Unpacking White Feminism," the history of White feminism is actually a history of "choosing one's Whiteness over one's womanhood." Carrie Chapman Catt, one of the original suffragettes in the first wave of feminism, appealed to Southern men by writing, "White supremacy will be strengthened, not weakened, by woman suffrage." She was right. White women betrayed women of color by offering to join forces with the White men in charge, enabling the number of powerful Whites to grow. Even today, White women continue to vote against policies and candidates that push us toward equality. Any relief I feel after racist and unjust politicians lose is always owed to Black women voters.

It took a string of betrayals by several White men for me to begin to recognize this issue. So many of these men who I placed my trust in let me down. But, in their failure, I became aware of two things. First, my belief in them had helped sustain and empower them. Second, I had benefited from my proximity to them. So when they lost privilege and position, I did too.

I realized that I needed to explore gender the same way I had explored race on Sankofa—and to move forward, I needed to start looking at the history of White women in America. I began reading and studying, which led me to challenge myths I held around White women's innocence and goodness. Even so, I couldn't see it clearly all by myself. There were many Black women in particular who helped open my eyes.

One of these women was Isabel Wilkerson, who writes in her book *Caste*,

> Slavery was not merely an unfortunate thing that happened to Black people. It was an American innovation, an American institution created by and for the benefit of the elites of the dominant caste and enforced by poorer members of the dominant caste who tied their lot to the caste system rather than to their consciences.

Another of these Black women was Stephanie E. Jones-Rogers, who writes in her book *They Were Her Property*,

> Slave-owning women not only witnessed the most brutal features of slavery, they took part in them, profited from them, and defended them. . . . For them, slavery was their freedom. They created freedom for themselves by actively engaging and investing in the economy of slavery and keeping African Americans in captivity.

Slavery was freedom for White women. Those who believed in a supremacist hierarchy and wanted to dominate in a racial caste as White women could do so. Slavery helped position them just under the White men in society. In many instances, it was the only way White women could acquire wealth or independence or any sense of power based on the laws and traditions of that era. All this time I had thought of slavery as being a White male-dominated institution when, really, many of its upholders and biggest fans were White women.

We don't have to go back decades or centuries to find examples of White women dehumanizing others for their own gain. We see White women in the news or on social media after they are caught on camera shouting, accusing, and threatening Black people who are minding their own business bird-watching, barbecuing, and tending to their own homes. We are assured that these White women who are acting up— "Karens"—should be scoffed at and distanced from the majority of "good" White women. "Karens" are the "bad apples," always seen as the exception and not as they truly are: woven into the fabric of Whiteness, because the power they abuse is accessible to any White woman at any time.

While Black girls are being trained to put their hands up immediately when pulled over by the police, White girls learn to appear oblivious, flirt, and play up our innocence and sexuality. Except the stakes are not the same. One of us is trying to get out of a speeding ticket; the other is trying to get out alive.

In her book *Hood Feminism*, Mikki Kendall writes:

Too often, White women decide that when they feel uncomfortable, upset, or threatened, they can turn to the patriarchy for protection. Because they don't want to lose that protection (dubious as it is), they stand by when it's convenient, and challenge it only when it directly threatens them. Yet, they know they benefit from it being challenged, and thus rely on others to do the heaviest lifting.

We are some fair-skinned fair-weather feminists.

To simply avoid "being a Karen" is an incredibly low bar. And the bar is practically on the floor when we compare ourselves to most White men . . . or is it?

I once sat in a meeting where the leader of the organization, a White man in his early sixties, looked over the document our team had created to train our staff. We sat in his office, which was rare for people in our positions. One entire wall held an impressive library with several best-selling books written by this leader. I think we all felt a tad intimidated and had high hopes he would be impressed with our presentation.

We were halfway through the document when someone read the word *power* aloud. He interrupted, insisting he didn't mean to be rude. "Is *power* really the word we want to put here? That is a very loaded word, and any time I'm in a conversation on race, things are going great until someone brings up the 'p-word.'" He asked our team leader for her pen, and we all watched as he crossed the "p-word" off his sheet and replaced it with the word *greed*. Then we looked at each other and followed suit. The irony that we all crossed off the word *power* as we witnessed exactly how power plays out is not lost on me. But as I've sat with that memory and turned it over again and again, there is more to it.

I could ask, "Why did he mansplain and cross off the word *power*?"—but maybe the harder question, and the one that's even more telling, is why did I let him? Why did I cross it off, too? Why did I think it wasn't my job to challenge his thinking in the moment? What was I afraid of? It didn't matter that I didn't agree when I complied. My fear and social conditioning were in the driver's seat. I was practically embodying the words of Alice Walker, that "the most common way people give up their power is by thinking they don't have any."

I told myself that I was being strategic, choosing my battles. That was true, but I was also afraid of being seen as disloyal and disruptive. I was afraid I wouldn't be seen as "one of them" but instead as difficult or combative. I was afraid I would create a wedge between myself and those whose opinions mattered most in my job and for my sense of belonging to the institution. But I'm starting to realize that what's scarier than what might happen to me when I speak up against Whiteness is what happens if I don't.

Looking back, so many of my memories of racism are tied to White women. A White woman instructed me to follow two Black shoppers. A White woman told us on the Sankofa trip that there were "good slave owners." A White girl told Katrina she had bugs in her hair. A White woman told me she hated how Black girls' hair smells. In many ways, White women taught me more about racism than anyone else in the world. In the words of another White woman, Ms. Britney Spears, "I'm not that innocent." It wasn't White men I needed to stop saying I loved from a place of defensiveness—it was *me*, especially when I acted out of fear of what might happen if I lost the approval and protection of White men *and* women with power.

Supremacy of any kind is power abuse. It's also power-hoarding. We collect all sorts of isms (racism, sexism, antisemitism, etc.) just in case we need to pull them out later. But these isms weigh on anyone who carries them and come at a cost, even if the cost seems invisible. When we turn to these isms to gain more power and dehumanize others, we are in turn dehumanizing ourselves. We don't get to ignore these power dynamics or wish them away. We have to understand them so we can name them in ourselves and in others.

Martin Luther King Jr. defined power as "The ability to achieve purpose and effect change." Power is not inherently bad or good. What matters is how power is used.

Brené Brown breaks down the use of power into two categories: power *over* and power *with*. "*Power over* occurs when we give people someone to blame for their discomfort, preferably someone who looks, acts, or sounds different than they do. *Power with* normalizes discomfort and moves away from shame and blame and toward accountability and meaningful change."

Supremacy of any kind is inherently power *over*, driven by fear. We fear because we don't believe there is enough, or that we aren't enough, or both.

We are in a crisis over power. So we must understand it to wield it for the greater good.

Kimberlé Williams Crenshaw famously introduced the term "intersectionality." She argued that none of us can be reduced to just one identity because we all experience different advantages and disadvantages due to a combination of social factors, including our gender, race, sexuality, religion, disability, and class. These overlapping social identities may be both empowering and oppressing. For example, a Black woman might experience privileges connected to accessibility that a White man in a wheelchair does not. Or a White undocumented person might be less likely to be asked for paperwork than a legal citizen of Latin

American descent based on racialized stereotypes. Intersectionality helps us better understand and expand on how power works. According to Crenshaw, "Intersectionality is a lens through which you can see where power comes and collides, where it interlocks and intersects."

A Black man I worked with at the church often brought up this question almost as a mind exercise: "Who has it harder here, a Black man or a White woman?" Back and forth we would discuss the church's history of segregation, cultural differences, barriers to education, and theological discrimination. Basically, we were asking, "Which ism is more powerful here, racism or sexism?" These questions get at the very heart of the intersectional conversation.

My Black girlfriends are not able to separate from these two isms. They often process experiences of discomfort, unease, and discrimination by asking themselves, "Did that just happen because I am Black or because I am a woman? Or both?"

We can't keep the work of antiracism only within the confines of race. It won't be fully understood or fully destroyed if we do. Many Black women during the civil rights movement were not respected or fully empowered due to sexism, and when these same women participated in the women's liberation movement, they were not respected or fully empowered due to racism. The solution is not to ignore the problems faced by Black women but just the opposite: we must center their voices, their experiences, their wisdom, and their creativity. In doing so, we get much closer to the center of both racism *and* sexism.

When we moved from Chicago to the suburbs, the real estate listing for our house began with, "Live at the corner of Comfort and Easy!" When we went to look at the house, we realized they were being literal. Now every day when I look out our living room windows, I see the signs marking the intersection of Comfort Street and Easy Street.

White men have set up residency at the figurative corner of Comfort and Easy. They have built all the other streets to serve this intersection and bulldozed any roads that tried to touch theirs. I am not saying life is always comfortable and easy for White men. But often, when life *is* comfortable and easy, it is connected to their Whiteness and their maleness.

If White men live at the corner of Comfort and Easy, White women live at the corner of Comfort and Hard. We share one street with the White men of the world and the other with women of color. None of us White women chose our intersection, but we get to decide which street we live on. We can choose to be accountable for the ways we've abused or ignored our power on Comfort Street. We can grow toward our own healing and wholeness as we face the real reasons we fought to stay comfortable, to stay solely on Comfort Street. We can choose to work alongside our sisters of color to make Hard Street more courageous, beautiful, and perhaps even a softer place to live.

Maybe my friend was right, there is something dangerous about someone who has access to the intersection of Comfort and Hard, of oppressor and oppressed. But what if we harnessed that power for something greater than hopes of making it to Easy Street? What if this could be our superpower, our version of power with? It won't be easy, but I bet it will be very good.

Start packing, White ladies. It's time for us to move—for good.

18

WHITE NOISE

So when people say that they don't like my tone, or when they say they can't support the "militancy" of Black Lives Matter, or when they say that it would be easier if we just didn't talk about race all the time—I ask one question: do you believe in justice and equality?

IJEOMA OLUO

But all our phrasing—race relations, racial chasm, racial justice, racial profiling, white privilege, even white supremacy—serves to obscure that racism is a visceral experience, that it dislodges brains, blocks airways, rips muscle, extracts organs, cracks bones, breaks teeth. You must never look away from this.

TA-NEHISI COATES

WHEN I FIRST STARTED MY RACIAL JUSTICE JOURNEY, I was twenty-one. The Civil Rights Act had passed forty years prior, and although racism hadn't been eradicated in those forty years (or the hundreds of years prior), I figured the end had to be in sight, that this problem would surely be solved in my lifetime. I thought people just hadn't yet learned about our nation's history, the American church's complicity, and the ways we were still perpetuating racial hierarchies and White supremacy. Was it just the naiveté of youth that I thought this way, or something else?

Growing up as a White kid during the 1980s, I was taught to be color-blind based on the baby boomer generation's bizarre and twisted inter-pretation of Martin Luther King Jr.'s "I Have a Dream" speech. So at twenty-one, I felt like I was discovering a new path—one that led me to be part of conversations, hear lectures, and read books discussing the topic of racism that had been strategically absent from much of my life. The further I traveled, the more I discovered this path was not only not new but one Whiteness never wanted me to find at all. The myth of colorblindness I had once easily swallowed I now found myself choking on. It was a tool to keep me and other White people from seeing color or race as anything but an extension of our own experiences—to only see racism with a capital R and not the subtle and subversive ways it perme-ated our lives.

Once I stopped reciting from the colorblind script I had been handed, I started hearing new lines from White people in response.

"I'm so tired of talking/hearing about race."

"It used to be so much worse. Why aren't people grateful that we're making progress?"

"You know, I think it's actually kind of racist to bring up the inequality—it just further perpetuates division."

"This is just some 'woke police' or 'PC types' looking for problems with anything."

"How can I be a racist if I'm married to/friends with/have a child who is a POC?"

"I wasn't alive two hundred years ago when slavery existed—why are you holding something I didn't have anything to do with over me?"

"It's a sin issue, not a skin issue."

These responses surprised me at first, but after a while I almost antic-ipated them. The unoriginality became predictable.

In college, I studied Ivan Pavlov's famous dog experiment. By leading dogs to associate the sound of a bell with being fed, Pavlov ultimately got them to salivate at just the sound of the bell, no food required. It was a breakthrough experiment that proved that a conditioned (or expected) response could be achieved with enough repetition. This became a much more important concept to me when I started sleep training my kids. The books tell you to memorize a repeatable script with the exact words you're going to say to let your baby know it's time to go to sleep. This process conditions the child to pair the words he hears with the response of going to sleep. (It works in theory. Sleep training was hard for us.)

Similar to the sleep training script, White people often approach the topic of racial inequality with the goal of quieting things down. The statements they make do not open up a dialogue in which someone's pain and experience can be shared and cared for. They are meant to shut things down, to get people to go back to sleep and return to ignorance.

I call this White noise. It is often a conditioned response (sometimes intended) to an uncomfortable or challenging conversation on racism. It's basically an "Ah, I bet you never thought of it this way" strawman argument. It is used to confuse, stump, and frustrate, effectively halting the exchange of ideas in conversation.

We have one of two choices: we can all be lulled back to sleep by the White noise, or we do whatever we can to stay awake.

This kind of White noise is not only harmful and problematic for communities of color. White people perpetuating White noise is a big deal. In fact, White noise spreads most easily in all-White spaces. So when racist ideas enter those spaces, however subtly, everyone can either agree that those ideas are allowed in the group, or they can dissent and say, "This is not who I want us to be." It's easier to shut it down the first time. Racism should not be given second chances.

So why does it sometimes feel risky to speak up against White noise even when we know what's at stake? There are various reasons.

We risk our sense of belonging. If we speak up and stand out from the group or family or institution, we risk being either kicked out or punished. Dealing with either of these possibilities may be painful, but we must consider whether our unchallenged complicity in racism is worth avoiding interpersonal pain. Ultimately, it's worth asking a deeper question—what are you willing to risk in the pursuit of racial justice and healing? It may include the status, the security, and the sense of protection once provided.

I have absolutely lost a sense of fitting in with many White people, but I would be remiss not to acknowledge all that I have received. As I continue to gain confidence in my activism and use my voice with growing frequency, I have been surprised at the sense of purpose and belonging I have found even as I stand apart from others. I have a deep sense of belonging to myself, to my community, and to my humanity. And rare was the time I stood alone for long. Conformity begets conformity, while courage begets courage. Be brave first and just watch what happens.

We don't feel "ready." There's a line from the popular children's book *We're Going on a Bear Hunt* that our family has memorized after reading it so many times. A family comes across all sorts of obstacles as they go on a walk outside, and each time they recite, "We can't go over it. We can't go under it. Oh no! We've got to go through it!" White noise, color-blind ideology, and silence are all tactics we use to avoid—to go under, over, and around. The only way we will ever be ready to confront racism in our circles of friends and family is by just taking that first step. We start where we are, with what we know, and begin. It's that simple. We make it hard when we try to guess where that first step will lead us and what it will reveal about how much we don't know or how much more work there is to do. That thinking slows us down. That longing to control the journey keeps us from starting at all.

We can be heard even as our voice shakes when we first speak our beliefs. We can be heard when we ask for more accountability and progress from our leaders. We can be heard when we challenge and disrupt the status quo—from our White family's house to the White House, from the boardroom to the school board, and from the school-to-prison pipeline to the Keystone Pipeline.

We learn by doing. We get stronger by doing. It gets easier by doing.

We're afraid we will make a mistake. This one is the hardest for me personally. Author Joseph Chilton Pearce has wise words for us, especially when the chance of making a mistake feels likely: "To live a creative life we must lose our fear of being wrong." To live a life of integrity and justice, one that challenges the status quo and isms of any kind, we must lose our fear of being wrong. It is holding us back.

In her wonderfully insightful way, Elizabeth Gilbert pragmatically names the power of fear:

> Fear is boring, because fear only ever has one thing to say to us, and that thing is: "STOP!" . . . Fear never has a more interesting insight to offer. Never. Just that one word, repeated and repeated with increasing hysteria: "STOP STOP STOP STOP STOP!!!!!" My fear wants me to stop, because my fear wants me to be safe, and my fear perceives all motion, all inspiration, all work, all activity, all passion whatsoever as potentially life-threatening. My fear wants me to live a smaller life. The smallest imaginable life, ideally. My fear would prefer that I never got out of bed.

Unchallenged fear is one of the most powerful aspects of being human. It is absolutely worth paying attention to, and it is absolutely not worth letting it dictate our lives.

It still stings to admit: I am not perfect. Never have been, never will be. I say this with all the gentleness I know how to use toward myself (especially as an Enneagram Type One, "the perfectionist," who longs for the ideal). You aren't perfect, either. It's worth poking at—why do we want to be perfect so badly? I personally sought perfection as a protective shield or as a way to hide, almost like using Harry Potter's invisibility cloak. But we do not get to hide behind perfection in this work of antiracism. Something perfect does not ever examine itself, ever grow, or ever evolve.

Fear and perfection want to keep us asleep in bed, cozy with control. Fight it. In the long run the cost of inaction is almost certainly more dangerous than the cost of making a mistake.

We don't know what to say. After 9/11, the expression "If you see something, say something" was everywhere. I took this very seriously.

From subway stations to movie theaters, I was on high alert. I once sat on a boat ride in the Great Barrier Reef convinced something terrible was going to happen as I watched a man behave "suspiciously." Then I watched him throw up; he was clearly just a tourist experiencing seasickness.

I think we've been taught that we'll witness racism on the scale of a shocking terrorist attack. Undoubtedly, that can happen. But I've more frequently seen racism expressed through "just a joke" or an "oversight in policy or procedure." If we spend all our energy gearing up for the big moments, we miss the "small" things that have the potential to continue unchecked and snowball into a bigger issue. It might seem as if taking a stand with those in your social network doesn't really matter—but if not you, who? And if not now, when?

This might come as a surprise, but I actually hate confrontation, and debating makes me sweaty. For a long time, I waited for those bigger, unmistakably all-caps RACIST moments before I would speak up. I rationalized that my energy was well spent on convincing people caught in obvious moments of racist behavior to change their ways. But I've found that speaking up isn't about convincing someone with a winning argument—it's about setting a moral boundary. My speaking up ensures that my opinion is known and that there is no silence to be taken as acceptance. It's not about others' reactions; it's about my action. To start with, "I disagree" is enough. Then you could say something like, "I'm not here to argue, but I ask that you respect me by no longer talking about this/talking this way around me. It's hurtful to people I care about and the values I hold, so it's hurtful to me also."

Here are some other sentences you can use:

"Please stop."

"That's not okay with me."

"I don't think that's funny."

"Is that what you really think?"

"Help me understand what you just said."

"That makes me uncomfortable."

We don't think our voice matters. What difference does it make if I speak up? I mean, really. I'm just one person.

A number of years ago, John and I were driving home after visiting some friends in Wisconsin. Both boys had fallen asleep in the back seat, so we turned off the kids' podcast and sat in the quiet for a bit.

"I'm thinking of writing about Sankofa," I said. "About how important it is to speak up." In her book *I'm Still Here,* Austin had shared the story of me saying, "Doing nothing is no longer an option for me," including the way people had resonated with my words on the bus. "I think I need to spend time thinking through that experience more."

"That sounds great, babe," John said. I wasn't surprised at his support. John is one of the most justice-minded people I have ever known. I learn so much from him. And he saw firsthand how Sankofa acted as a catalyst for change in both our lives.

I asked John if he ever thought back to that trip.

"Yeah, I think about it. I'm obviously so glad you said what you said, and it clearly meant so much to people on the bus. But when I look back and think about the few White people sharing ignorant comments, I feel like most of the rest of us on the bus knew that what they were saying was nonsense."

"Okay—but no one was saying anything not full of nonsense except for the Black students."

I was not doing a good job of keeping my voice out of kid-hearing range. I considered asking him to pull over so we could get out and talk without fear of disturbing naptime.

My heart began to race. Why would anyone assume that those White students' silence meant anything but their complicity? Why would anyone assume that our silent thoughts were any better than public excuses, distancing methods, and White noise? On that bus, we had just spent the last forty-eight hours confronted with some of the worst things humans could do to other humans—why would anyone give the White people the benefit of the doubt at that moment? Or frankly, ever?

"You're right," John said. "There's a reason I didn't speak up—I assumed people knew where I stood in response to those comments. But, obviously, they didn't. Which is why it mattered so much when you did."

I felt my heart rate return to normal as he reached to hold my hand.

It's easy to think that as long as we're not agreeing with every racist idea or comment, we're somehow off the hook. But it's not clear where we stand unless we say it out loud, even when it feels unnecessary. Speak up constantly, and don't rest on what you said last time. Then say it again just to be sure it sticks. Nowhere you go is off-limits—the grocery store, your child's school, the doctor's office, your place of worship, the neighborhood block party, the family picnic, your office conference room, the playground, your high school reunion, your father's retirement party, the PTA, your book club . . . you get the picture.

Because if we don't go head-to-head to quiet White noise, it will get louder and louder until it ultimately drowns out everything within its reach.

19

DEAR ABBI

MY FRIEND ABBI AND I HAVE KNOWN EACH OTHER since high school. After Elliot was born, she came over with two bags full of clothes that her toddler had outgrown. She taught me how to make boy clothes cuter ("It's all about adding a cool shoe") and was the kind of mom who showed up to playdates with a messy bun paired with bright lipstick. She's cool without trying to be. I adore her.

She and I have often circled back to topics of racism, faith, feminism, and politics. We grew up at the same church and both departed from the colorblind rhetoric we had been handed as White women. In our conversations, she shows curiosity and a deep desire to better understand the world and her place in it that I have always admired.

We met recently for drinks at my favorite cocktail bar, Common Good (appropriately named for our discussion). Conversations like this—without our kids running around interrupting status-quo-disrupting thoughts—were rare, and it felt nice to go deeper than our time together usually allowed. Which was needed since I had a bit of an agenda.

"You are exactly who I hope resonates with this book I'm working on," I admitted to her in between sips of my drink. "I know you think about this stuff a lot, and we've been talking about it for years. But what are you sitting with? What feels confusing or hard?"

Abbi asked questions that felt familiar and common and real. It wasn't the first time I had heard them or even asked them myself. It got me thinking. "Will you send me more questions, or even just what you're sitting with after tonight?" I asked as we stood in the parking lot. I didn't know what I would do with what she shared, but I wanted to keep the conversation going and the questions coming. The next day, she sent me the first of what would be many messages. I've included some here and other parts of our conversations from that night.

My hope is that we would all be encouraged to have more conversations like this with each other. And let me be clear who "each other" is, as I hear from many White people who believe they need people of color in their lives to talk about racism with. You don't! In fact, if you aren't having these conversations as a White person with other White people first, that's your first step (and maybe your second and third). This is not a guide for what those conversations should look like, but it is what our series of conversations contained.

As an aside, I have always loved advice columns. The curious part of me enjoys peeking in on people's problems and the advice columnist's approach for giving guidance. When I realized I was talking to a friend named Abbi, I couldn't help but think of the famous "Dear Abby" column. This title is meant to be playful and does not suggest that I am the "expert" in our friendship, or that these questions have a single answer, or that my answers are the best or only ones out there. I'm grateful Abbi has welcomed me into her journey and that she's not doing the work of antiracism alone.

● ● ●

Hey Jenny,

The big thing I keep thinking about is having a framework for boundaries. We touched on this the other night when you said, "People entrenched in their own racist beliefs (even if they are close to you) aren't your main work—your kids are." That's the kind of distinction I get really confused about. I hear, "White people, go get your people," and that's what can overwhelm me. I can't burn every bridge in my life. I can't always get into big conversations about everything, so it's either I do that or I do nothing.

Should I just be focusing on having explicit conversations with my kids and making resources available if people ask? And what about my community? Do you have rules in your mind for what you engage with and what you don't? When you don't have that, it's easy to get really overwhelmed and then just burn out.

Dear Abbi,

There is so much to unpack in just these few sentences. First of all, thanks for your willingness to trust me with these questions. You are not alone in them, and I want to preface my response by saying I am on this journey with you and my responses are likely to evolve the more I learn myself.

Let's start with the framework. Many White people who feel completely overwhelmed by the enormity of racism and how much they never knew want to launch right into solution mode. Which is why one of the most common questions we hear from White people is "What should I do?" When we ask that about every little and big thing, it exposes a lack of overall philosophy or foundation, and likely a lack of clear boundaries. It can be easy to spend a lot of time and energy starting with what feels like the most overt or blatant racism. And it can be easy to hear a directive like "White people go, get your people" and think that means we just need to go head-to-head with our most outwardly racist family member or neighbor. But that is not our main antiracism work. I say this because focusing only on what's hardest doesn't help build momentum. That doesn't mean we're off the hook and we should never pursue it. Instead, our priority should be what is closest to the center of our spheres (who lives in our house) and what is a daily occurrence (what institutions we participate in), especially at the beginning. Quite simply, I think we should start with what is most accessible to us.

As a mom, you know what books are being read in your home, what conversations you are having around the dinner table, and what values you are prioritizing through your family's time and money. That is a very natural place to start. Build from where you are and what you know. Look at what's right in front of you: your kids, your job, your family, your community, your place of worship, yourself. And as you look at yourself, pay attention to what you are drawn to and what you care about—what is sustainable to keep you anchored in the work for the rest of your life. Start there, and you will slowly move further away from what's closest or most comfortable.

Those anchors are key to my own framework in how I first began to engage. The work became more personal and approachable when I took stock of what aspects energized me and what helped me move from an *I should* to an *I get to* mindset. I'm not saying it will never be hard, but I don't think it should always feel so heavy.

When John and I lived in DC, there was an unusually large and mighty speedbump across the street from the rowhouse I rented. People would often miss it, and the sound of cars smacking against the pavement became common until an older neighbor took it upon himself to stand on the sidewalk and yell at drivers as they passed. "Watch the hump!" he shouted over and over again. He became devoted to his message and could be seen standing guard on most days. It worked. Cars would slow down and avoid any damage. It became an inside joke between John and me. "Watch the hump!" we would say in passing, knowing it could elicit a laugh as we emphasized the last word. So I say to you now, "Watch the hump." Watch for things that cause you to lose momentum. Watch for things that threaten your commitment and do lasting damage. Maybe also watch for where the system is broken and needs a sign put up to warn others!

My rules are pretty simple: I engage in things that keep me committed and evolving in the work. For me, that's less debating over thought exercises, and more demanding reform and abolition of institutions that were designed to work in a cruel and racially unjust way. For me, that's less convincing White people who don't see racism in their everyday lives, and more accountability with committed White folks and people of color. For you, that might mean something really similar or really different. There is no one-size-fits-all antiracism plan. It is incredibly personal and unique to who you are. I love this from the Jewish text found in the Talmud: "Do not be daunted by the enormity of the world's grief.

Do justly now, love mercy now, walk humbly now. You are not obligated to complete the work, but neither are you free to abandon it."

PS. I don't think burning bridges with family members will necessarily make the world more just, nor is it required to pursue antiracism. No one is beyond hope of transformation and change. I have seen powerful changes occur in people through relationships (myself included). So while change is possible in others, the only person we have control over changing is ourselves. What is doable is to have boundaries (i.e., you don't debate people's humanity, you have no tolerance for hate speech or slurs, etc.). That means not all behavior will be allowed in your presence, and certain subjects might need to be off-limits if they push past your boundaries. If there are signs that people in your life really are curious or interested, you don't have to ignore them. Engage wisely. Send them a book or article to read that's been helpful to you and see if they are up for discussing it. That could be a great sign that they are genuinely interested and that it's worth deeper engagement. But we have limited energy, and you and I are both raising White boys in a culture ushering them into toxic masculinity and White supremacy; maybe that can be enough to focus on at first (in addition to ourselves, of course).

Keep going,
Jenny

● ● ●

Hi, Jenny. What do you do when you are processing and looking back at racist things from your past that make you cringe? About eight years ago, I was at a dinner with coworkers and I asked everyone what their ethnic background was to fill some awkward silence. People went around the table and then it was the last person's turn, a Black coworker. She said she didn't know because her ancestors were enslaved and that's how they were here. I got so flustered and could only respond with, "Right, of course." I felt so ignorant. I hate thinking about it and how on-the-spot I put her and how I kept talking because it was awkward. When I told my cousins this story years later, they were like, "You are not racist, stop feeling bad about yourself." I didn't intend to be racist, but upon reflection much later, I realized I was. And I don't think I'm a bad person; I was ignorant, and that's probably part of this coworker's experience all the time. I've always struggled with what to do with this—do I contact her and apologize, or does that make it about me because I feel really guilty about it? What do we do with the missteps we've made?

Dear Abbi,

I think it's really important to sit with the parts of our story we cringe at, less from a position of judgment and more from a place of curiosity. To hold it up at different angles and thoroughly examine it. Because so often, we don't. We let ourselves off the hook (in your case, your cousins did that for you), or we start to shame-spiral. There is no chance for growth or changed behavior where there is no reflection, and we can't reflect when we're defending, deflecting, or spiraling.

These moments reveal what we're capable of. But they do not wholly define who we are. I hear from you a deep desire to, as Maya Angelou put it, "know better, do better." So now that you know better, what should you do? And should you do anything?

I don't know if this former coworker would like an apology, nor do you. So perhaps you could start by taking stock of your history. Consider the relationship dynamics, whether you're still in relationship with the person, and the consequences of not repairing the relationship, versus having not spoken to someone for years but feeling the urge to clear your conscience. Is this the first time you two have directly talked about racism—about her experience as a Black woman or yours as a White woman? If the answer is yes, sit with that. The least amount of harm might be leaving her alone.

If you do reach out, I would ask at the very beginning if she would be open to a conversation/apology about the incident. Give her some agency over this situation. What you've been carrying for years might be something she doesn't even remember or want to revisit. If she is open to connecting, I would come prepared with an apology script.

We've come up with one in our family: "I'm sorry for (blank). I shouldn't have (blank). Next time, I'll (blank). Can you please forgive me?" The "next time" is so important because it shows that you've thought through the next time. You are taking your mistake and learning from it, not just for self-reflection but for changed behavior.

There was an anonymous quote trending on social media last year that, in my opinion, we should all memorize: "We're not accepting verbal apologies this year, only changed behavior." In this instance, you could say something like, "Next time, I will bring the understanding that my relationship to my past contains privileges others don't have the same access to—that what for me is a fun icebreaker could actually be a source of deep pain and trauma for someone else. I will think about that person before I speak and ask a different question." There are many other ways you could express your changed behavior, but hopefully, that helps.

No one likes an "I'm sorry, but . . ." apology. That makes it more about you than about her. The point is not to make you seem like a good person or a nice White woman. The point is to take ownership of pain and potentially provide a path toward healing.

If you express remorse and she is unable to forgive you, that could be really hard to accept, but it is absolutely her prerogative and a natural consequence of being someone she may only see as unsafe. There are consequences for our actions, and a loss of deeper or healed relationships with other people is one of them. Regardless of ever sharing that apology with her, you need to complete that script for yourself. Carrying it around is not doing anyone any good. I don't think enough people understand how much grace and forgiveness are required when it comes to racial justice—and not from the people we've harmed directly and indirectly, but from ourselves for ourselves. Otherwise, we run the very real risk of staying stuck. A great way to shut growth down is to beat yourself up. As Anne Lamott puts it, "Not forgiving is like drinking rat poison, and then waiting around for the rat to die."

We will never be perfect. And we can always be better.

Keep going (imperfections and all),

Jenny

● ● ●

Hey, Jenny. We celebrated Juneteenth by getting food from a Black-owned restaurant, but later, I was reading social media posts that said, "This holiday isn't for White people," and I felt so confused. I know it's not a monolith—people are always going to have differing opinions, but how do you come to conclusions while staying open to feedback?

And I don't know if I'm just worried about what people think of me or if I want to be prepared and informed if someone challenges what I'm saying or doing. I don't have the capacity to know everything, but that shouldn't keep me from taking steps in my life toward antiracism. That's where I get stuck.

Dear Abbi,

At the church I used to work at, the one service we could never seem to make everyone happy with was Mother's Day. Every year, we would receive lots of criticism. We either didn't acknowledge how hard it is being a mother or how incredible and joyous it is. One year, we acknowledged mothers and grandmothers but forgot single moms, stepmoms, and those trying to get pregnant. One year, we just had all the women stand up to be acknowledged. It was too much for one day to hold. The more we tried to see everyone, the more we diluted it and had a hard time seeing anyone fully—especially the people the day was actually intended to celebrate.

The same thing can happen on a day like Juneteenth, a day of celebration inextricably tied to incredible grief. Juneteenth can never be experienced the same way for both White and Black people. We do not possess the same claim to the day, the history, the culture. Does that mean White people can't acknowledge, be educated on, and financially support that day? I don't think so. But it does not belong to us and it never will. To be really blunt, not everything is for White people. We don't get to rejoice that freedom from slavery was won while we held the keys to the oppressed people's chains throughout history, and, in many ways, still do to this day.

You are absolutely correct that Black people are not a monolith; they will have different perspectives and philosophies and experiences and opinions. It's imperative to seek out people of color who are teaching on antiracism and listen to them most closely. Follow them on social media, subscribe to their newsletters, read their books, and attend their workshops. Pay them. If they aren't addressing the exact question you have, Google it and see what Black, Indigenous, Latinx, and AAPI folks are saying. You will notice that, while they likely don't agree on everything, they share certain values. Give those the most attention. When I feel confused, I remind myself to "major on the majors, minor on the minors." If they are all in agreement on something, that feels like a major. And don't get stuck feeling bad that you don't automatically know this stuff already.

Not knowing everything is never the reason to stay quiet. A White know-it-all on race is not the goal. Our education on racism as White women will never outweigh the lived experiences and perspectives of those most oppressed by racism. But we have to know some things, so what do you need to *know* so you can have the confidence to *do*? And, maybe even more importantly, what steps do you need to take to be transformed into something better and make the world better? This work is not to make you feel superior or consider yourself a "nice" person, but to deepen your humility, making room for more humanity and, ultimately, freedom for all.

In your questions I hear a lot of things that are keeping you spinning instead of starting and sustaining. You mentioned when we met that it feels like some people want you to have a position on everything. I think you need to be building a strong foundation, rooted in history and context and those trusted antiracist voices. Otherwise, you will get frustrated as you constantly try to reinvent the wheel. I too have been so afraid of being told I'm doing things wrong. But I've learned over the years that when people correct you, they still have hope for you. Do not fear it. Too often, I've feared the wrong things. But over time, I started to be less afraid that I didn't know enough or that I would appear racist, and I became more concerned about what racism does to humanity and what it does to me. I don't do this perfectly, but when I remember this, it helps realign and clarify my focus.

Also, we must try to avoid caring about rules the most. We think the rules will make us better allies, but they actually keep the focus on us. How can we see what's right and wrong in the world when we are focused solely on whether *we* did something right or wrong? Being an ally can quickly spiral into being all about you, and that is much too narrow in scope if we are trying to change anything in the world.

This work has the potential, like you said, to be overwhelming and burn us out before we even really begin. We can't stay where we've been, but we should get curious about why we've been there for so long. What if we started with some core questions like, "What have I learned and unlearned? What do I know now that I didn't used to? Where have I been that's kept me from learning and unlearning? What's different now? What do I want the world to look like? If I have learned about how systems keep Black and Indigenous people especially marginalized and oppressed, what are some natural next steps I can take?"

We will find what we should do and be better equipped to do it for the long haul—small doing over big and "perfect" thinking.

Keep going and growing,

Jenny

20

WRITE YOUR OWN VOWS

Many people take on antiracism as something to learn about. And that's partially true. Learning alone isn't the process. Education and knowing more isn't the end goal. Freedom and equity and full humanity are. Book clubs have dropped off. People have unfollowed the antiracism educators they followed last summer. What's missing? Embodiment of the work. When you're not actively embodying anti-racism, it is harder for it to take root. Our actions and who we are in the world flow from our embodiment. What does that mean? Embodiment is not a mysterious process. But it does not happen overnight . . .

JESSICA DICKSON

MY HUSBAND AND I HAD OUR FIRST DATE ON A SNOWY, slushy Chicago February night. We took the L train downtown to Michigan Avenue, browsed the books at Borders (RIP), feasted on milkshakes and French fries, and capped our night with the Spike Lee film *25th Hour*.

Years later, we loved learning that Michelle and Barack Obama's first date had also included the viewing of a Spike Lee joint—the classic and evergreen *Do the Right Thing*. I won't spoil anything if you haven't seen it, but let's just say "doing the right thing" is complicated. Even in the movie.

And yet, it's what so many people seem concerned with in regard to issues of racial injustice: getting it right. And, even more pervasively, not getting it wrong by avoiding mistakes in an attempt to not look stupid, racist, or uneducated.

As I mentioned, I am a Type One on the Enneagram. No one loves and craves perfection like us. So I get this to my very core. And yet, over time—because of enough times of getting it right-ish or wrong-ish—those arbitrary goal lines shift so that instead of doing the *right* thing, it's more about doing the *growth* thing.

Another snowy night in Chicago, just six years later, John and I were driving from the city to the suburbs to meet with our wedding officiant and her husband. She served spicy enchiladas and margaritas, which made us forget about the blizzard outside. Somehow the topic of our pre-marital counseling session turned to the subject of divorce and why this couple was starting to see friends around them splitting up.

It was happening to enough of their friends that they spotted a few patterns. One was that couples weren't both growing as individuals, or growth was not happening toward each other.

There is often an unspoken idea that if you are "working" on your marriage or relationship, it's a bad sign. "But, of the couples I know that have the types of relationships others look at with envy, they are working their butts off for that kind of connection and growth," our wedding officiant said. "Be more like them. That's the best advice I have for you two. Here's to commitment, growth, and working our butts off."

We laughed, clinked our glasses, took a final sip of our now-watery margaritas, and said our goodbyes. I've returned to this moment many times since that night.

That September, in a flower shop in the city, I walked down the worn wood aisle toward John. I faced him and the witnesses there that night to make vows of commitment, growth, and work—all rooted in the love we had found together. We were reminded that these vows were not the conclusion of our journey but the next chapter in our love story.

That was over a decade ago, and while I don't remember every detail of that day, it is an anchor point in our marriage. Speaking those words alone is not why we've stayed married. But those words gave language to a vision for a life together, and a promise and commitment to that vision.

A few years later, when we started the conversation on trying to get pregnant, John and I found ourselves on different pages. I was terrified we would have trouble conceiving like my mom did. He was terrified children would strain our marriage. At counseling, we were invited to examine vows we hadn't spoken to each other that September night— vows we hadn't realized we had each made, rooted in fear and scarcity and discomfort. To move forward, we had to name those unspoken vows and commit to breaking them, and then replace them with new ones.

We all have unspoken vows. Maybe you have an unspoken vow of safety, of comfort, of fitting in. Maybe you have, consciously or not, vowed to "make it," to be successful, to do whatever you need to get ahead. Maybe you have vowed to do whatever you must to make your children's lives easier or more comfortable and secure than yours was growing up. Those aren't inherently bad things. But, like Brené Brown says, "We can choose courage or we can choose comfort, but we can't have both. Not at the same time."

If you say you care about justice issues, know that your vows to pursue both justice *and* comfort will battle each other. Like oil and water, they are incompatible. Pursuing justice is anything but comfortable, no matter how long you've been at it. And it requires a ton of courage.

You have to start breaking some of your unspoken vows.

You have to embody the vows that remain, and you might even need to write new ones. It will not happen overnight. And yet, it must start somewhere.

I can't tell you everything you should do. You're going to have to figure that out for yourself. My hope is that you write your own vows, imagine a vision for the world, and figure out your unique part in the creation of a better way. You will not know where each step leads, and that's okay. You start anyway. You hold up every area of your life and say to it, "Doing nothing is no longer an option." You get off the moving walkway and run like mad in the opposite direction.

I return to my vows again and again because they have expanded and changed over the years.

I keep at the forefront the reminder that I will not do this perfectly. Mistakes (especially ones where, if I can help it, only I get hurt) are welcomed. My goal is to never let my discomfort outweigh my commitment.

I am clear about the voices of friends and leaders I listen to most closely. Those are people who know me in real life, who aren't afraid of telling me what they think, and who can have a real conversation with me.

I try to pass the mic to amplify others' voices, give credit to them always, and be open to feedback. I stay aware of my place—of my own limitations as a White woman. I vow to stay humble, to not be a know-it-all, and to not rush to validate my own position or opinion.

I am clear about who and what this work is for. It's never to make me feel better as a White woman. It's to do what I can to make the world better for all.

Our family pays reparations. We have a line item in our monthly budget to keep us accountable. I financially support those I'm learning from as well as Black, Indigenous, Asian, and Latinx artists, writers, organizations, and businesses. A shoutout is not the same as a check.

I don't take up spaces not meant for me. I will not be solo leading your company's next diversity, equity, and inclusion workshop (but I would love to make suggestions for who can).

I try to do my work as much as possible "beside and behind"—in collaboration with and in support of people of color.

I start from a place of listening and learning but push myself to put what I've heard and learned into action.

I hold tight to the mantra "I can't do everything, but I can do something."

There are so many good and right questions to consider when you are faced with injustice and you realize you have a role to play. But we must move beyond only asking, "What should I do?" to make room for "Who do I need to follow?" and "Who do I want to become?" and "What do I want the world to be?" This is evidence of real, sustainable growth. If you want to be the best possible version of yourself, you will need to have a vision and a commitment to antiracism in your life. And isn't that a gracious byproduct of doing what's best for humanity, including what's best for White people? That we should get something even greater in return—embracing and living out of our own humanity?

There seems to be this myth that engaging in racial justice is similar to charity, with clear roles of server and those being served. But the chains of oppression are wrapped so tightly around us all. White people, White supremacy is coming for us too. It might be coming for others first, but make no mistake—when the cancer of hate and intolerance spreads and wipes everyone else out, it will not care how little melanin you have in your skin as it crushes those who lie in its way. This is happening in naked ways, such as White people being killed at the Capitol on January 6, 2021, and in more subtle ways, such as policies that keep guns easily accessible, leading to increases in mass shootings, domestic violence, and suicide rates, which particularly impact White men. The Department of Homeland Security declared, "White supremacists are the most persistent and lethal threat within the country." White supremacy impacts us all.

As I've reflected back on my time on that bus that quite literally changed my life, I've realized that was my first commitment ceremony. I walked down an aisle and made vows that would become a vision for how I needed to live my life. I looked at the faces of people I cared about, people who were witnesses to my words. My journey started there, and it continues to this day. Imperfectly and persistently.

May your good, hard, imperfect work be deeply rooted in love, bearing the fruit of justice, equality, imagination, restoration, healing, life, and a future. May there be joy in the resistance, magic in the collective, comfort for the disturbed, and a disruption for the comfortable.

And may you vow to do something, anything, every day, as long as you and the work of racial justice both shall live.

Do you vow that doing nothing is no longer an option?

I really hope your answer is "I do."

ACKNOWLEDGMENTS

FOR AS LONG AS I CAN REMEMBER, WHENEVER I START A BOOK, I turn past the first chapter and instead begin with the acknowledgments section. I love learning about the people who acted as doula to the birthing of whatever book I'm about to read. I could go on and on about the people in my own life who have made the birth of this book a reality. However my publisher has basically started the wrap it up music at the awards show so I should probably get going already.

My agents Alexander Field and Trinity McFadden at The Bindery Agency—thank you for your belief in my voice and encouragement from the very beginning.

My editor, Elissa Schauer, and the whole team at IVP—your guidance and wisdom made this book so much better. Thank you for understanding my vision and helping me sharpen and clarify it each step of the way.

To anyone who lent me their memories from shared past experiences or who cheered me on in any way, I appreciate you so much.

I'm so lucky that my early readers are some of my very best friends:

Abbi Togtman (thanks for letting me write a whole chapter about you!),

Alyse Liebovich (I'm crossing my fingers that a copy of this will show up at your library),

Ashlee Eiland (thank you for answering a million author questions and showing me how it's done),

Bridgette (thanks for being the center of so many inside jokes),

Caitlin Leman (no one I would rather be raising these wimpy White boys alongside than you, dear friend!),

Emily Norman (seared into my memory is your voice memo swearing a lot about this book and it makes me so happy—thanks for being my muse, the one I was almost always writing this for),

Hannah Eloge (thanks for pumping me up so many times and that one time you had champagne sent to my hotel room),

Katrina Foster (not only did you trust me with sharing our story, but your support of this book means everything to me),

Kylee Pantanella (your words "the world needs your words" were burned in my brain during times of doubt—thank you),

Meredith Miller (you were an OG early reader for a reason—thanks for pushing me and challenging me and sitting on Zoom calls brainstorming subtitles and, and, and),

Rhianna Godfrey (you are the best cheerleader—thank you for hyping me up because I know you really meant it).

Brenda Olsen and Sarah Springer—thank you for giving me space to process and wise counsel from the very moment the idea for this book popped into my head.

Some of the best teammates and collaborators a girl could ask for: Brooke Campbell, Stephanie McBee, Chi Chi Owku, Andrew Schuurmann, and Nick Benoit.

Austin Channing Brown—thank you for asking me to jump off mountains with you. The answer is always yes.

My family—especially my parents for so graciously encouraging me to write this book. And for taking me to the library so much growing up. And for sending me to Willow Bend Elementary.

Elliot and Milo—I am the luckiest to be your mom. And yes, Milo, you and Elliot are my darlings.

John—no one knows the highs and lows of book season quite like the author's partner. Thank you for marking the highs (with sushi, champagne, dance parties in the kitchen) and the lows (with pep talks and constant reassurance and the patience of a saint as you listened to me talk over and over through ideas). I quite literally could not have done this without you. Thanks, babe. I love you and I like you.

QUESTIONS FOR REFLECTION AND DISCUSSION

1. What is your earliest racialized memory? How do you feel about that memory today?

2. What does Sankofa mean to you in your life? In the story of your country?

3. How did you feel reading Katrina's story about the sleepover? Did anything surprise you about your reaction?

4. Have you ever been in a situation where you witnessed racism but stayed silent? Why do you think you chose not to say anything? Conversely, have you been in a situation where you did speak up? Was there a noticeable difference?

5. Martin Luther King Jr. said, "In the End, we will remember not the words of our enemies, but the silence of our friends." What do you think this means? How have you seen it in your own life?

6. Were you surprised by the study about how diversity strengthens teams? Why or why not?

7. What does being colorblind mean to you? Were you taught that growing up?

8. How did you feel when you read the story of the White woman admitting she was a racist? Pay attention to your body—what is its response?

9. Can you think of a time when you have witnessed tokenism?

10. It's one thing to reckon with the sins of America's past, but how are you reckoning with what is occurring in your lifetime? Do you agree with Jenny that "everywhere is a crime scene"?

11. What was the impact of the murder of Trayvon Martin in your life?

12. What institutions have you been a part of that have expressed concern for diversity?

13. How has knowing people of color changed you? Have you experienced grace in the pursuit of racial justice?

14. If you have kids, do you talk to them about racism? Why or why not?

15. In chapter sixteen, Jenny talks about situations that don't feel completely clear; they are gray areas. Can you think of any examples of situations that have felt gray to you?

16. Why do you think power is such a vital part of the issue of racism? Where can you use your own power to help fix what is broken?

17. What are some examples of White noise you have heard or said in your life?

18. Do you have friends you talk to about race? How often does it come up?

19. If you were to write your own vows, what would they include?

EXPERIENCES

1. Would you like to do your own marble jar activity? Here is the complete list of questions from our class:

   - The last three families you hosted in your home were:
   - The last three families whose homes you visited were:
   - The latest three magazines in your home are:
   - The last three meals you ate were:
   - The last three restaurants you visited were:
   - The style of art in your home is:

- The style of music played in your car is:
- The last museum exhibit you visited depicted:
- The last three movies you went to see were:
- The three most-played movies in your home are:
- The three most-played television shows in your home are:
- The people you sit next to in church are usually:
- The last three books you read are written by:
- Your two next-door neighbors are:
- The dominant culture in your neighborhood is:
- The newspapers you read regularly are by:
- The bloggers you read regularly are mostly:
- Most of your Facebook friends are:
- Your three closet friends are:
- Most of your coworkers are:
- Your family's dominant culture is:
- The schools you attended were:
- Most of your child's friends are:
- Most people in your small group are:
- The dominant style of music played in your church is:
- In the last play you attended, the cast was mostly:
- In the last two concerts you attended, the artists were:
- Other languages I speak represent:

2. Spend time journaling through your own personal laments and confessions. Perhaps share them with a trusted person.

3. Write a script of responses for when you hear White noise in your life.

NOTES

INTRODUCTION

6   *When we limit white to just a description of skin color*: Eve Ewing, "I'm a Black Scholar Who Studies Race. Here's Why I Capitalize 'White,'" *Medium*, July 2, 2020, https://medium.com/zora/im-a-black-scholar-who-studies -race-here-s-why-i-capitalize-white-f94883aa2dd3.

7   *Books are never finished*: Sreechinth C, "Oscar Wilde and his Wildest Quotes" (self-pub., Createspace, 2016), Kindle, 65.

1. WHITE GUILTY GIRL

15 *African Americans incarcerated at five times the rate*: E. A. Carson, "Prisoners in 2019," Bureau of Justice Statistics, October 16, 2020, https://bjs.ojp .gov/library/publications/prisoners-2019.

2. DOING NOTHING IS NO LONGER AN OPTION

21 *Because Black people have bugs*: Katrina Foster, personal correspondence with author, December 11, 2021.

30 *Reporting on lynchings*: Brent Staples, "When Southern Newspapers Justified Lynching," *New York Times*, May 5, 2018, www.nytimes.com/2018/05/05 /opinion/sunday/southern-newspapers-justified-lynching.html.

31 *Fifteen thousand men, women, and children gathered*: Isabel Wilkerson, *The Warmth of Other Suns: The Epic Story of America's Great Migration* (United Kingdom: Random House, 2011), 39.

3. "OMG KAREN, YOU CAN'T JUST ASK PEOPLE WHY THEY'RE WHITE"

43 *Bind us together*: Bob Gillman, "Bind Us Together" (Kingsway Thankyou Music, 1977).

    In the End: Martin Luther King Jr., "Beyond Vietnam—A Time to Break Silence" (speech), American Rhetoric, April 4, 1967, www.americanrhetoric .com/speeches/mlkatimetobreaksilence.htm.

4. Do You Want to Get Well?

46 *Every church should strive for racial diversity*: Bob Smietana, "Research: Racial Diversity at Church More Dream Than Reality," Lifeway Research, January 17, 2014, https://lifewayresearch.com/2014/01/17/research-racial-diversity-at-church-more-dream-than-reality/.

47 *Diverse groups are more creative*: Adam Grant, host, "The Daily Show's Secret to Creativity," *Worklife with Adam Grant*, March 7, 2018, https://podcasts.apple.com/us/podcast/the-daily-shows-secret-to-creativity/id1346314086?i=1000405268582.

48 *Moving walkway illustration*: Beverly Daniel Tatum, *Why Are All the Black Kids Sitting Together in the Cafeteria? And Other Conversations About Race* (New York: Basic Books, 2017), 115.

53 *Race is the child of racism*: Ta-Nehisi Coates, *Between the World and Me* (New York: Random House, 2015), 7.

When we attempt to be colorblind: Ibram X. Kendi, *How to Be an Antiracist* (New York: Random House, 2019), 54.

5. Losing My Marbles

57 *You don't need to be the thief*: Tori Williams Douglass (@ToriGlass), "You Don't Need to be the Thief," Twitter, May 30, 2021, https://mobile.twitter.com/toriglass/status/1399163139703201794.

58 *White blessing*: Sarah Pulliam Bailey, "Q&A: Rapper Lecrae on His Discomfort with Hearing Slavery Described as a 'White Blessing,'" *The Washington Post*, June 16, 2020, www.washingtonpost.com/religion/2020/06/16/qa-rapper-lecrae-his-discomfort-with-hearing-slavery-described-white-blessing/.

59 *Whiteness is a constantly shifting boundary*: Paul Kivel, *Uprooting Racism: How White People Can Work for Racial Justice* (Gabriola Island, BC: New Society Press, 1996), 19.

Shame is a tool of oppression: Austin Channing Brown, Chi Chi Okwu, Jenny Booth Potter, and Brené Brown, "Brave Together," November 5, 2019, in *The Next Question*, produced by Austin Channing Brown, video web series, 1:11:48, www.tnqshow.com/season-1.

6. Insert Token to Play

66 *Calling out workplaces supposedly doing the most good*: Helen Kim Ho, "8 Ways People of Color are Tokenized in Nonprofits," *Medium*, September 18,

2017, https://medium.com/the-nonprofit-revolution/8-ways-people-of
-color-are-tokenized-in-nonprofits-32138d0860c1.

69   *Racism requires those in power*: Ho, "8 Ways."

To discount race: Sheree Atcheson, "There Is No Race Card to Play Because
Race Is Intertwined Into Everything," *Forbes*, January 15, 2021, www.forbes
.com/sites/shereeatcheson/2021/01/05/there-is-no-race-card-to-play
-because-race-is-intertwined-into-everything/?sh=7d851d6d5cc7.

7. EVERYWHERE IS A CRIME SCENE

77   *Y'all raping our women*: Emily Shapiro, "Key Moments in Charleston Church
Shooting Case as Dylann Roof Pleads Guilty to State Charges," ABC News,
April 10, 2017, https://abcnews.go.com/US/key-moments-charleston
-church-shooting-case-dylann-roof/story?id=46701033.

8. THE VERDICT

83   *Letter from Birmingham Jail*: Martin Luther King Jr. and Jesse Jackson, *Why
We Can't Wait* (United Kingdom: Signet Classic, 2000), 72.

9. A CONFESSION

89   *As if he gave the "I Have a Dream" speech*: Austin Channing Brown, Chi Chi
Okwu, Jenny Booth Potter, and Andre Henry, "Power to the People," October
13, 2019, in *The Next Question*, produced by Austin Channing Brown, video
web series, 40:05, www.tnqshow.com/season-1.

10. HANGING BY A THREAD

93   *Nearly 60 percent*: David Mendieta and Samuel Carlson (July 2021), "Esti-
mate of Homeless People in Chicago (2015-19)," Chicago Coalition for the
Homeless, www.chicagohomeless.org/estimate.

Divided by Faith: Michael O. Emerson and Christian Smith, *Divided by Faith:
Evangelical Religion and the Problem of Race in America* (Oxford: Oxford
University Press, 2000).

The most segregated hour: Martin Luther King Jr., interview by Ned Brooks,
Meet the Press, NBC, April 17, 1960, https://kinginstitute.stanford.edu/king
-papers/documents/interview-meet-press.

94   *We are integrating into a burning house*: Harry Belafonte and Michael
Shnayerson, *My Song: A Memoir* (New York: Alfred A. Knopf, 2011), 328-29.

11. Amazing Grace

97   *The margins as holy places*: Kaitlin Curtice (@KaitlinCurtice), "Imagine that: the margins as holy places. The world turned upside down," Twitter, July 10, 2017, https://twitter.com/KaitlinCurtice/status/884496381049790464.

99   *I am not free*: Audre Lorde, "The Uses of Anger" (speech), National Women's Studies Association Conference, Storrs, Connecticut, June 1981, www.blackpast.org/african-american-history/speeches-african-american-history/1981-audre-lorde-uses-anger-women-responding-racism/.

103   *The best criticism*: Richard Rohr, *Things Hidden: Scripture as Spirituality* (United Kingdom: SPCK, 2016), 74.

13. Raising White Parents

107   *Two hundred fifty years*: Ta-Nehisi Coates, "The Case for Reparations," *The Atlantic*, June 2014, www.theatlantic.com/magazine/archive/2014/06/the-case-for-reparations/361631/.

14. Wimpy White Boys

117   *Wimpy White Boy Syndrome*: David G. Oelberg, "WWBS: Fact or Fiction?," *Neonatal Intensive Care* 27 no. 2 (March–April 2014): 8, www.nicmag.ca/pdf/NIC-27-2-MA14-R4B-web.pdf.

119   *Suicide deaths*: Centers for Disease Control and Prevention, "Web-based Injury Statistics Query and Reporting System (WISQARS) Fatal Injury Reports," February 20, 2020, https://webappa.cdc.gov/sasweb/ncipc/mortrate.html; Neil Watkins, "Men and Suicide: Why Are White Men Most at Risk?" *Baton Rouge General*, July 1, 2021, www.brgeneral.org/news-blog/2021/july/men-and-suicide-why-are-White-men-most-at-risk-/.

      Mass shootings: John Haltiwanger, "White Men Have Committed More Mass Shootings than Any Other Group," *Newsweek*, October 2, 2017, www.newsweek.com/White-men-have-committed-more-mass-shootings-any-other-group-675602.

      These men suffer: bell hooks, *The Will to Change: Men, Masculinity, and Love* (United Kingdom: Atria Books, 2004), 138.

120   *Eight times as much political power*: Nia-Malika Henderson, "White men are 31 percent of the American population. They hold 65 percent of all elected offices," *The Washington Post*, October 8, 2014, www.washingtonpost.com/news/the-fix/wp/2014/10/08/65-percent-of-all-american-elected-officials-are-white-men/.

120 *Fortune 500 CEOs*: Halla Tómasdóttir, "The Inclusion Revolution in Leadership: Changing Who Leads Will Transform How We Do Business," *Fortune*, April 28, 2021, https://fortune.com/2021/04/28/leadership-inclusion-revolution-c-suite-boardroom-diversity/.

We don't encourage boys to be whole: hooks, *The Will to Change*, 12.

The experience of wholeness equips us: Hugh Mackay, *The Good Life* (Australia: Pan Macmillan Australia, 2013), 65.

121 *Black-sounding names*: Payne Lubbers, "Job Applicants With 'Black Names' Still Less Likely to Get Interviews," *Bloomberg*, July 29, 2021, www.bloomberg.com/news/articles/2021-07-29/job-applicants-with-black-names-still-less-likely-to-get-the-interview.

123 *Most White parents find the term endearing*: Oelberg, "WWBS: Fact or Fiction?," 8.

Gender is performed: Judith Butler, interview by Max Miller, "Your Behavior Creates Your Gender," BigThink, January 13, 2011, https://bigthink.com/videos/your-behavior-creates-your-gender/.

15. "MOMMY, WHO IS GEORGE FLOYD?"

129 *Sesame Street survey*: J. A. Kotler, T. Z. Haider, and M. H. Levine, *Identity Matters: Parents' and Educators' Perceptions of Children's Social Identity Development* (New York: Sesame Workshop, 2019), www.sesameworkshop.org/what-we-do/research-and-innovation/sesame-workshop-identity-matters-study.

131 *Broadening the joining*: Audre Lorde, *Sister Outsider: Essays and Speeches* (New York: Clarkson Potter/Ten Speed, 2012), 11.

Clear is kind: Brene Brown, "Clear is Kind, Unclear is Unkind," October 15, 2018, https://brenebrown.com/articles/2018/10/15/clear-is-kind-unclear-is-unkind/.

135 *If we lived in a diverse society*: Jennifer Harvey, *Raising White Kids: Bringing Up Children in a Racially Unjust America* (Nashville, TN: Abingdon Press, 2019), 51.

140 *White middle schoolers*: Rebekah Gienapp, *Raising Antiracist Kids: An Age-by-Age Guide for Parents of White Children* (Rebekah Gienapp, 2020), 50.

141 *Extremist recruiters understand*: Caitlin Gibson, "'Do You Have White Teenage Sons? Listen Up.' How White Supremacists Are Recruiting Boys Online," *Washington Post*, September 17, 2019, www.washingtonpost.com/lifestyle/on-parenting/do-you-have-white-teenage-sons-listen-up-how-white

-supremacists-are-recruiting-boys-online/2019/09/17/f081e806-d3d5
-11e9-9343-40db57cf6abd_story.html.

16. THE GRAYNESS OF BLACK AND WHITE

143   *Dressing up as Black Panther*: Jen Juneau, "Cultural Appropriation or Not?
Parents Speak Out About Black Panther Halloween Costumes," *People*,
October 8, 2018, https://people.com/parents/black-panther-halloween
-costume-cultural-appropriation-debate/.

The differing opinions: Kwame Opam, "The Many Meanings of Black Panther's Mask," *New York Times*, February 13, 2018, www.nytimes
.com/2018/02/13/style/black-panther-children-costumes.html.

17. ON THE STREET WHERE YOU LIVE

150   *White feminism*: Rachel Cargle, "Unpacking White Feminism," speech, pre-
sented at the Bodhi Spiritual Center, Chicago, IL, February 23, 2019.

Woman suffrage: Carrie Chapman Catt, "Objections to the Federal Amendment," in *Woman Suffrage by Federal Constitutional Amendment*, ed. Carrie
Chapman Catt (New York: National Woman Suffrage Publishing Co., 1917),
76, https://awpc.cattcenter.iastate.edu/2018/03/21/woman-suffrage
-by-federal-amendment-chapter-vi-objections-to-the-federal-amendment
-jan-1917/.

151   *Slavery was an American innovation*: Isabel Wilkerson, *Caste: The Origins
of Our Discontents* (New York: Random House, 2020), 44.

Slave-owning women: Stephanie E. Jones-Rogers, *They Were Her Property:
White Women as Slave Owners in the American South* (United Kingdom: Yale
University Press, 2020), IX, XVII.

152   *White women decide:* Mikki Kendall, *Hood Feminism: Notes from the Women
That a Movement Forgot* (New York: Penguin Publishing Group, 2020), 166.

153   *The most common way*: Alice Walker in Guy Dauncey and Mary-Wynne Ash-
ford, *Enough Blood Shed: 101 Solutions to Violence, Terror and War* (Canada:
New Society Publishers, 2006), 56.

154   *The ability to achieve purpose:* Clayborne Carson, *The Autobiography of
Martin Luther King, Jr.* (New York: Grand Central Publishing, 2001), 353.

Power over, *power* with: Brené Brown, "On Power and Leadership," Brené
Brown (website), October 26, 2020, https://brenebrown.com/wp-content
/uploads/2021/10/Brene-Brown-on-Power-and-Leadership-10-26-20.pdf.

Intersectionality: Kimberle Crenshaw, "Kimberlé Crenshaw on Intersectionality, More than Two Decades Later," interview, Columbia Law School,

June 8, 2017, www.law.columbia.edu/news/archive/kimberle-crenshaw
-intersectionality-more-two-decades-later.

18. WHITE NOISE

161   *To live a creative life:* Joseph Chilton Pearce, "Joseph Chilton Pearce Quotes,"
       BrainyMedia Inc, accessed April 11, 2022, www.brainyquote.com/quotes
       /joseph_chilton_pearce_159486.

       Fear is boring: Elizabeth Gilbert, "Your fear is boring," *Elizabeth Gilbert*
       (blog), October 4, 2014, www.elizabethgilbert.com/your-fear-is-boring
       -i-can-say-this-with-all-honesty-and-authority-because-i-k/.

19. DEAR ABBI

171   *Not forgiving:* Anne Lamott, *Traveling Mercies* (New York: Anchor Books,
       1999), 134.

20. WRITE YOUR OWN VOWS

177   *We can choose courage:* Brené Brown, *Rising Strong: How the Ability to Reset
       Transforms the Way We Live, Love, Parent, and Lead* (New York: Random
       House Publishing Group, 2017), 4.

179   *White supremacist threat:* Tal Axelrod, "Homeland Security Report Released
       After Months-Long Delay Lists White Supremacists as 'Lethal' Threat," *The
       Hill*, October 6, 2020, https://thehill.com/policy/national-security/519908
       -homeland-security-report-released-after-months-long-delay-lists.